The Glucose

Revolution Approach

Unlock the Secret Methods to Manage Blood Sugars,

Reverse Insulin Resistance, Lose Weight and Restore

Your Health- Plus Diabetic Meal Plan Ideas and

Food Journal

Marilyn Phillips

From the Author

As you read this book, *Glucose Revolution*, envision a path to vitality and well-being. The journey to achieving your set goal transcends scales and glucose monitors; it's a celebration of your body's incredible resilience. In the *Meal Plan* section of this book, with every recipe, you will find nourishment for both your body and spirit. Each mindful choice, is a step towards balancing your blood sugar. With this book you're not just shedding pounds; you're shedding limitations, embracing a life infused with energy and joy. This isn't merely a guide; it's a companion on your road to optimal health. Diabetes and weight loss are but chapters in your narrative—rewrite them with resilience and self-love. Trust the process, honor your body, and savor the sweet taste of well-being.

-Marilyn Phillips

TABLE OF CONTENTS

INTRODUCTION

Millions and millions of Americans suffer from diabetes, however, just 1 in 4 are aware that the disease can lead to serious complications like blindness, kidney failure, and amputations. So, don't you want to know how to control your blood sugar if you have diabetes or are pre-diabetic?

Your body works hard to maintain a healthy level of blood sugar. As soon as you eat that bowl of pasta or cookie, your pancreas begins to release the hormone insulin to metabolize the sugar you've consumed. When you have too much sugar in your blood, your blood gets thick and syrupy, which is unhealthy. Just imagine how much extra work your heart has to do to pump viscous blood throughout your body. In the next few hours, a blood sugar spike will induce a sugar rush, subsequently followed by a sugar crash, with all of the associated cravings and fatigue. Repeated blood sugar spikes can lead to heart problems, renal problems, eye issues, and nerve disorders such as neuropathy, which results in losing feelings in your fingers and toes.

When you consume too much sugar, the calories mount up and your body needs more insulin to break down all of the sugar. After a while, the pancreas will be unable to keep up with production, which may lead to insulin resistance, prediabetes, Type 2 diabetes, and heart problems. Excess sugar and caloric intake lead to weight gain and contributes to an array of more medical conditions such as high blood pressure, high cholesterol, and obesity.

There isn't a single, foolproof method for lowering blood sugar naturally; rather, managing diabetes requires a multifaceted approach even once it is fully under control. For instance, exercise is crucial since it supports the maintenance of a healthy body weight and a healthy BMI. Additionally, it aids in fat loss, particularly belly fat, which is linked to poor insulin sensitivity or diabetes. Supplements may also be necessary, but use caution— they can be problematic. Since many of them are not FDA-approved, you must ensure that you utilize them exclusively under supervision. To lower your blood sugar, you need also to learn how to manage your stress. Naturally, you want to keep your blood sugar levels in check, but stress also raises stress chemicals like cortisol, which can elevate blood sugar. Make sure to visit your doctor for advice on managing your diabetes. It's critical that you understand what diabetes is and the causes of elevated blood sugar. Knowing the symptoms of diabetes in particular will be very beneficial to you. How do you get off the rollercoaster? It primarily comes down to making several vital lifestyle changes, starting with what you eat, for otherwise healthy people (who do not have diabetes). The smart hacks in this book will help you control your blood sugar and feel better while staying healthy.

Section I

SUPERFOODS FOR BLOOD SUGAR CONTROL

Learn about natural ways to reduce blood sugar with superfoods.

Green Super Foods

I'm going to share with you how eating the following green superfoods will help you keep your blood sugar levels in check and enhance your general health. A major concern for millions of people globally is high blood sugar and it can be challenging as well as terrifying to manage your blood sugar while attempting to enjoy meals, but worry not—nature has you covered. Consuming these greens can help your body absorb glucose and improve your insulin sensitivity. They also contain essential vitamins and minerals that are needed for other biological processes in your body. Green superfoods have been specifically created to contain specific nutrients and compounds that work in synergy with our body's natural processes, including blood sugar regulation.

Cucumber

This non-starchy vegetable may already be your favorite salad, but it can help you fight high blood sugar. In fact, according to a 2016 study on the potential preventive effects of cucumbers for diabetics, it is a perfect diet for glycemic control and can help reduce diabetes-related problems. So, aside from being a member of the gourd family, let's get to know the cucumber better. A 100g of cucumber has only 15 calories and virtually no fat, but it is packed with antioxidants such as vitamins C and K that can prevent diabetes. Additionally, it is a good source of potassium, manganese, and magnesium—minerals that support the heart. Did you know that vitamin C has been shown to reduce post-meal blood sugar levels?

A vital component of eye health, vitamin K also helps to fortify bones. To be more precise, it might help lower the risk of age-related macular degeneration caused by diabetes. Potassium is essential for the proper functioning of the heart and is needed for the metabolism of carbohydrates. Other potent antioxidants contained in cucumbers include flavonoids, lignans, and triterpenes. Studies have shown that lignans and flavonoids reduce inflammation and enhance heart health and blood sugar regulation. According to studies, triterpenes can lower cholesterol, enhance liver health, and generally protect against oxidative stress. Cucumber seed extract and cucumber pulp have been shown in animal studies to aid diabetic lab rats in reducing their blood sugar levels and improving their overall glucose management, so include this green food in your next blood sugar-balancing salad.

Okra

Who ever thought that one of the easiest ways to naturally reduce blood sugar was to eat some good old okra? Although it is commonly processed and prepared as a vegetable, okra is classified as a fruit loaded with tiny round seeds and known for its mushy and slimy feel. It is a staple meal in many cultures and thrives best in hot, humid areas. It can be pan-roasted, grilled, steamed, or boiled. Moreover, it can be included in sautés, stews, and soups. However, what effect does okra have on blood sugar levels? According to randomized research conducted in 2022, participants who consumed 100mg whole food capsules of okra for eight weeks saw a significant drop in their HbA1c levels when compared to the control group. The study revealed that okra had promising antihyperglycemic effects for those with type 2 diabetes. According to the Journal of Medicinal Plants in 2017, lab rats that were fed okra had significant reductions in blood sugar levels. But precisely how can this seedpod aid in lowering blood sugar levels? According to studies, its greater insoluble fiber content may cause the digestive tract to absorb blood sugar more slowly. Okra also provides a wide range of beneficial vitamins, such as vitamins A, C, and K, along with B6 or pyridoxine and B9 or folate. Magnesium, which has been shown to improve insulin sensitivity and reduce the risk of type 2 diabetes, is among the antioxidant micronutrients that are abundant in okra. Folate may lower the risk of cardiovascular diseases and is involved in the production of red blood cells. It has been discovered that pyridoxine helps maintain brain health and may lower the risk of age- and diabetes-related cognitive disorders. Meanwhile, 100g of okra has only 33 calories, so why not give it a try? When you eat okra, especially if you eat it frequently, it can help to lower your blood sugar naturally, which is why if you are already diabetic and on diabetic medications, please consult with your physician because okra is a potent way to lower blood sugar naturally.

If the slimy texture turns you off, try other ways of preparing it; you might discover that it has become your new favorite green food.

Avocado

Not only is it one of the finest green foods for blood sugar regulation, but it's also pretty much everyone's favorite. They have a rich, creamy texture, and their high-fat content may lead you to feel that this gourmet meal is simply too rich for your blood, but eating adequate amounts of avocado can help with heart health and glucose management. According to research, avocado has no substantial detrimental influence on blood sugar. Snacking on a small amount of avocado can help reduce cravings for unhealthy foods. A randomized trial conducted in 2022 on persons who were overweight or obese revealed that eating avocado for 12 weeks resulted in healthier eating habits that supported better glucose regulation. The study also discovered that eating avocado reduced biomarkers of cardiovascular disease in participants. But how do these high-fat fruits do all of this despite being rich in fat? That might not be such a bad thing after all, since the majority of the fat in avocado is heart-healthy monounsaturated fat, mainly oleic acid. This fatty acid has been associated with lowering of blood pressure and cholesterol, enhanced heart health, less inflammation, increased weight loss, and a lower risk of certain kinds of cancer. Meanwhile, a full avocado contains 14g of fiber, which is roughly half of your daily recommended consumption for this important glucose-lowering, hunger-reducing food. Still, half of a small avocado provides roughly 4.6g of fiber, so a little can go a long way towards stabilizing your post-meal blood sugar, preventing unhealthy cravings, and improving your digestive health. According to a recent study, participants who were overweight, and ate roughly 150g of avocado daily for 12 weeks experienced lower fecal bile concentrations and higher bacterial diversity compared to those who did not eat avocado. Given the significant role the gut microbiome plays in the metabolism of both carbs and fats, gut health is crucial for those with high blood sugar. Avocados also contain phytosterols, which have been shown to lower total and LDL cholesterol by limiting cholesterol absorption in the intestines. While this green fruit is high in calories and fat, eating a modest portion of it a few times per week can help with satiety, weight management, heart health, and blood sugar balance.

Kiwi Fruit

To begin with, let us address one of your primary concerns regarding fruits, their sweetness. Diabetics are advised to limit their consumption of meals with a glycemic index of 70 to 100. Ripe bananas, watermelons, pineapples, mangoes, and dried dates are among the fruits that fit into that category. A delicious green kiwi, on the other hand, has a GI score of 50. It belongs to the low glycemic group as a result. A 100g serving of kiwi contains 64 calories, 3g of fiber, and 14g of carbs. Kiwi fruits have a small amount of protein, which means they can help to decrease digestion and post-meal glucose absorption. Kiwi is also a great source of antioxidants, such as vitamins C, E, and K, that fight diabetes. Folate, copper, magnesium, and potassium are also abundant in kiwis. Vitamin E may lower heart disease risk factors; vitamin K helps maintain eye health and is especially important for older diabetics who are at risk of macular degeneration; and vitamin C not only strengthens the immune system but also lowers the risk of inflammation and studies suggest it can aid in post-meal glucose stabilization. Consuming adequate levels of magnesium has been shown in studies to reduce the risk of developing type 2 diabetes. The antioxidant carotenoids lutein, zeaxanthin, and beta-carotene, which are associated with a lower risk of macular degeneration, oxidative damage, heart disease, and certain types of cancer, are also abundant in this fruit.

Kiwi fruits also contain potent polyphenols such as chlorogenic acid and caffeic acid, which have been shown to lower inflammation while improving the health of the gut. So, don't be afraid to incorporate this fuzzy green fruit into your daily diet, and if you can stomach it, eat the skin since it contributes to the overall fiber content.

Edamame

A cup of these beans offers just 224 calories and 37 of your necessary daily requirements of digestion delaying plant-based protein. A cup of edamame also contains 8g of dietary fiber, which can help with your post-meal blood sugar levels. Edamame's high fiber content also contributes to its low glycemic index ranking. Furthermore, high in antioxidant micronutrients such as calcium, copper, folate, iron, magnesium, phosphorus, potassium, riboflavin, thiamin, and vitamin K. Vitamin K, magnesium, potassium, folate, and folate have all been linked to improved insulin sensitivity and heart health. Nerve conduction, cell growth, and heartbeat regulation are all associated with phosphorus. The body uses thiamin to make adenosine triphosphate (ATP), a molecule that transports energy within cells, copper helps maintain a healthy immune system, riboflavin can lower oxidative stress, and calcium not only strengthens bones and teeth but has also been shown to protect against type 2 diabetes, high blood pressure, and certain kinds of cancer. So, incorporate this green powerhouse into your diabetes-fighting diet now for better control of blood sugar levels in the future.

Other Non-Starchy Veggies

Non-starchy vegetables are a natural method to reduce blood sugar. But when it comes to starches and carbohydrates, this isn't the case. Carbohydrate is a string of glucose that takes the form of polysaccharides. Consuming a lot of starchy carbohydrates, such as those found in bread, rice, potatoes, etc., can cause your body to absorb the sugar more quickly and raise your blood sugar levels, which is bad for managing diabetes.

Make sure to include a variety of non-starchy veggies, like *Asparagus*, in your diet. I'm a big fan of asparagus because it tastes great, is low in calories, is packed with folates, and can be prepared in a variety of ways to satisfy your appetite without having all of the excess calories. This means it can also help you maintain a healthy weight, which is another natural strategy to lower your blood sugar.

Broccoli is another non-starchy vegetable that has numerous health benefits. It can help you lose weight by naturally lowering your blood sugar. Broccoli is also high in vitamins and antioxidants, and it can help boost your immune system naturally.

Artichoke is another fascinating-looking non-starchy vegetable. To get to the actual artichoke component that you may eat, you must first remove all of the artichoke's gorgeous delicate-looking bits on the outside to reach the center, the heart of the artichoke. If you're someone who's moving around busy and doesn't have time to do that, you can look for places where all the work has been done, all of its excess leaves have been pulled off. But you still need to be careful when you find one. When you do find one, though, you still need to apply caution. If an artichoke heart appears to be soaked in any preservative, be sure it's actually simply water, or if it's just oil, consider using some virgin olive oil. Take caution when doing so since you don't want to raise your cholesterol or do anything that might cause severe inflammation.

If you aren't going to consume these veggies fresh, make sure to cook them as little as possible to preserve the most amount of nutrients.

Green Leafy Vegetables

Spinach, kale, and collard greens are low in calories. They are high in vitamins, antioxidants, and beta-carotenes, and eating more of them can help you reduce the amount of unhealthy foods you consume, maintain good blood sugar levels, maintain a healthy weight, and maintain greater insulin sensitivity. Therefore, eating plenty of leafy green veggies is still another excellent natural method of lowering blood sugar.

Again, there is no one magic cure for diabetes; rather, there are numerous foods that can help you reduce your blood sugar levels naturally. See your doctor or dietitian for advice. It is not always simple to maintain a healthy lifestyle and eat all of these healthy foods that help lower your blood sugar naturally.

Red Super Foods

When it comes to nutrition, red isn't just any old color. Naturally, red foods are rich in minerals, vitamins, and antioxidants as well as other potent micronutrients that promote general health. Red foods have several general health benefits, such as decreasing blood pressure, protecting the body from free radicals, preventing certain kinds of cancer, improving heart health, and perhaps most importantly—lowering blood sugar.

The red color in these foods is mainly due to antioxidants, such as anthocyanins, which have been shown to help with diabetes management. Let's get to this list because there is much more to red foods than meets the eye.

Rhubarb

It is impossible to overstate the importance of eating fruits and vegetables that are low in carbs yet high in fiber. This spring vegetable is high in vitamin K and is distinguished by its vibrant pink to red stalks and dark green leaves. This antioxidant has been found to lower blood pressure by preventing mineralization in the arteries. According to a 2020 study, taking vitamin K regularly may improve insulin sensitivity and lower the risk of diabetes. However, red rhubarb contains a variety of important diabetes-fighting antioxidant micronutrients such as vitamins A and C, calcium, folic acid, magnesium, manganese, and potassium. It was even discovered in a 2018 Taiwanese study that rhubarb stem extract improved the fasting blood sugar of diabetes patients; for this reason, rhubarb essential oil is now suggested as an additional treatment to help lower blood sugar levels. Nonetheless, we recommend eating rhubarb fresh, as its tart flavor complements salads well. If you want to add some spark, try fresh rhubarb and salsas or roast them for a dinner side dish. It's also a tasty addition to smoothies and homemade juices. This red vegetable is often paired with another red fruit, the strawberry, to prepare a delectably rich strawberry and rhubarb pie. However, this may not be an ideal choice for people who are concerned about their blood sugar levels, so just watch how much sugar you add to your pie and think about using a nut-based pie crust to cut down on the amount of carbohydrates overall. When buying fresh rhubarb, look out for stalks that are long and crisp; (to get them, they are usually at their finest from April to June) just be sure to remove the inedible leaves before eating and enjoying this red amazing blood sugar lowering veggie.

Dragon fruit

Dragons may be a myth, but dragon fruit is a real-life wonder. These stunning deep magenta fruits grow from a cactus plant known as pitaya and have a somewhat sweet and floral taste, the pulp inside is velvety with small black seeds, and you may eat the pulp seeds and all. Fruits of all kinds provide natural sugars, but eating fresh fruits, such as dragon fruits, also provides a wealth of dietary fiber that helps to slow down the response of your body and digestion. Due to its low glycemic index—between 48 and 52—dragon fruit is a great fruit option for diabetics because it won't significantly raise blood sugar levels. Additionally, dragon fruit contains a high vitamin C content, which has been demonstrated to support vascular health and may help reduce blood sugar levels after meals. A 2017 study linked eating dragon fruit to improved glycemic management. According to the study, eating dragon fruit regularly may help delay the onset of type 2 diabetes. Studies on dragon fruits conducted on animals also show that they contain antioxidant carotenoids like beta- and lycopene, as well as the ability to promote the formation of pancreatic cells, which produce insulin in the body. These red-colored compounds in dragon fruit have been shown in studies to lower the risk of heart disease and several types of cancer. This fruit also contains more antioxidants than other red pigments, which have been shown to protect against the oxidation of harmful LDL cholesterol. Peel off the outer skin of the dragon fruit before preparing it. This fruit can be added to a summer salad or enjoyed as a diabetic-friendly snack. It's also a tasty addition to diabetic fruit salsa. Cubed dragon fruit can also be blended as a sweet but fiber-rich addition to your morning smoothie.

Red wine

You shouldn't be surprised to find red wine on the list because red wine has long been known to provide health advantages when consumed in moderation. It turns out that it is beneficial not just for heart health but also for diabetics. Drinking certain alcoholic beverages, particularly red wine, has been demonstrated to lower blood sugar levels for up to 24 hours, according to the American Diabetes Association, and other studies show that moderate red wine consumption can help reduce your risk of developing type 2 diabetes. So how does this work? Red wine contains a variety of polyphenols, including catechins, epicatechin, and the now-famous resveratrol.

These antioxidants can protect blood vessel linings, as well as aid in intestinal health, protect against the development of certain kinds of cancer, lower LDL cholesterol, and reduce the risk of heart disease. Red wine's naturally occurring polyphenols have been shown to naturally assist with insulin sensitivity and post-meal glucose control by inhibiting the intestinal absorption of glucose. Moderate alcohol consumption has been shown in studies to enhance insulin secretion and thereby lower blood sugar levels. But what precisely is moderation?

Women may consume up to one small glass of wine each day, while men may consume up to two. Drinking too much can also seriously harm the pancreas, so you should take extra care to limit the amount of red wine you drink and the frequency with which you drink it. Additionally, steer clear of wine spritzers, which have a lot of added sugar. It is also recommended that you monitor your blood sugar levels before consuming your preferred red wine, as the sense of intoxication can be akin to feelings of hypoglycemia, or potentially deadly low blood sugar levels. Red wine can also be more regulated in its effects if you take it with meals.

Red Chili Peppers

For those who enjoy spicy cuisine, there's good news for you: red chili peppers can lower blood sugar levels. According to a 2018 study, eating peppers, mostly for their hot bioactive component capsaicin, can assist in better managing metabolic syndrome and its linked conditions such as diabetes. The results of the study demonstrated that capsaicin improved glucose homeostasis regulation in type 2 diabetes patients and reduced insulin resistance. Recently, capsaicin has also been used as a primary ingredient in topical creams since research suggests it may help with diabetic neuropathy discomfort. Red chili peppers also contain capsanthin, a keratinoid pigment that gives these peppers their red sheen. This antioxidant has been shown in studies to have anti-inflammatory, anti-obesity, and anti-diabetic properties. Meanwhile, red chili peppers have a variety of additional heart-healthy blood sugar-balancing micronutrients such as vitamins A,

B6, C, and K, potassium, and copper, so don't be surprised. According to a 2006 study, those who ate a spicy meal that included these peppers had reduced blood sugar levels. That same study also found that those who added up to three tablespoons of chili pepper to their meal experienced significantly lower blood sugar levels at the end of the day, so don't be afraid to sprinkle delicious red chili flakes, red chili pastes, or simply a sprinkling of freshly chopped red chili pepper to your favorite spicy dish.

Cranberries

These small, tart red spheres pack a nutritional punch and help regulate blood sugar levels. Cranberries are classified as a superfood since they are high in antioxidants, particularly vitamin C (as previously stated, vitamin C can help your arteries). New studies suggest that it might aid in lowering blood sugar levels after meals. They also contain potent diabetes-fighting micronutrients such as vitamins E and K, copper, and manganese. Additionally, it includes a naturally abundant supply of polyphenols, an antioxidant that has been found to help reduce fasting glucose levels and enhance insulin sensitivity. Beneficial flavonoids included in cranberries also support glucose metabolism, which makes it easier for your body to process glucose. One cup of unsweetened cranberry juice, consumed daily for 12 weeks, significantly reduced the serum glucose levels of participants, according to a 2012 study published in the Journal of research in Medical Sciences. But the term "unsweetened" is crucial in this case. Choose your cranberry juice wisely at the grocery store, staying away from products that have added sugar. If you don't want to take the risk with juice, it's still far better to eat the whole fruit to reap the benefits of blood sugar-stabilizing fiber. Cranberries can be eaten whole as a diabetic-friendly snack, added to salads, or even served as the main ingredient in your morning's unsweetened yogurt. You can even freeze them so you'll always have them at hand any time of the year.

The Top-6 Super Foods
Spices

Yes, they're all in your cabinets. You've probably seen them in the grocery aisles. Although there are many more spices, we are particularly going to talk about turmeric, cinnamon and garlic.

Cinnamon: It should come as no surprise that cinnamon is a spice derived from tree bark. There have been many studies but sometimes it's hard to compare because different doses have been used. Cinnamon was found to have no clinically significant effect on blood sugar in certain research, but several studies have demonstrated that there is a clinically major distinction so you should definitely speak with your doctor. One study, for example, examined those who took 1, 3 and 6g of cinnamon every day. The blood sugar levels in those groups were significantly lowered in that particular study when they were compared to individuals who received a placebo and did not utilize any cinnamon at all. Another study was conducted with 69 type 2 diabetic patients in China; the patients were compared to those who did not use cinnamon daily, and the results showed that the cinnamon users had lower triglycerides in addition to lower blood sugar. That being said, it's important to practice caution not to use excess cinnamon, 6 grams or fewer should be used daily, if you intend to take a cinnamon supplement (because that can result in specific issues), additionally, keep in mind that supplements may not be FDA-approved. In summary, there are inconclusive results from several studies. A meta-analysis of ten studies on cinnamon found that again, some studies reported a significant lowering, while others did not. The key takeaway is that it may help, and won't hurt, but speak with your doctor first because cinnamon may be a natural approach to lower your blood sugar.

Turmeric: This is another spice to consider. It is a well-known spice, and if you haven't heard, curry turmeric contains curcumin, which is responsible for color and flavor and helps with inflammation. Turmeric is a well-known antioxidant and spice that has anti-inflammatory properties. Studies have shown that turmeric can help decrease cholesterol, and blood sugar, and aid with chronic inflammation. This is only one of many spices that, in various situations, can aid in naturally lowering blood sugar.

Garlic: It has numerous medicinal properties, including the ability to naturally reduce blood sugar levels. Garlic has components that are rich in both vitamins and antioxidants. Some studies suggest that it can help to naturally lower blood pressure, triglycerides, and blood sugar levels. A review study conducted in 2015 found a clinically significant difference in fasting blood sugar reduction between individuals who took garlic and those who did not. Another research study conducted in 2018 also found this same pattern. Patients in this study crushed raw garlic twice daily and were compared to individuals who did not use the garlic. They were compared to the placebo group, and once again, there was a substantial difference in blood sugar levels. Those who consume garlic have lower blood sugar levels as well as a smaller waist circumference. In addition to having decreased triglycerides, they lost a greater percentage of body weight. As previously mentioned, it's crucial to speak with your doctor because some studies have been conducted that are a little less conclusive. However, keep in mind that garlic is a food that may help to naturally lower your blood sugar.

Pumpkin

Pumpkin is a beautiful orange winter pumpkin that can naturally help reduce blood sugar levels. Pumpkin is low in calories and high in fiber, with a low glycemic load that differs from the glycemic index. Glycemic load refers to the amount of sugar absorbed from carbs into the bloodstream. A glycemic load is deemed favorable when it is less than 10. The glycemic load for pumpkin is less than three, which differs from the glycemic index, which is quite high, therefore it's crucial to grasp all of the health benefits when dealing with pumpkin.

Fiber: They have 3 grams of dietary fiber per cup of pumpkins, but it's also important to understand that you do need to practice some portion control because, as I mentioned, even though they have a low glycemic load, they have a high glycemic index, and so if you start eating a lot of pumpkins, you could run into problems with your sugar.

Vitamin A: Pumpkins are rich in vitamin A, which is very beneficial for the health of your eyes. It lessens age-related macular degeneration. Moreover, it can lessen night blindness and cataract development. I am stating this because people with diabetes frequently experience these kinds of vision problems, therefore eating pumpkin in moderation can be beneficial.

Vitamin C: Pumpkins are also a good source of vitamin C, which reduces blood vessel inflammation. We know that many diabetics have inflammation in their blood vessels, which can lead to excessive cholesterol and, in turn, enhance the need for amputations due to impaired circulation. Thus, you should eat a lot of vitamin C-rich veggies. One such vegetable is the pumpkin. Now, when I say pumpkin, (all things pumpkin is not healthy) I'm talking about fresh pumpkin. For instance, you already know that pumpkin pie is high in sugar, and pumpkin puree may also be high in sugar. If you're looking for canned pumpkins or pre-prepped pumpkin seeds, they may be high in salt and am not even talking about pumpkin lattes that are also loaded down with sugar as well. Therefore, you should cook with fresh pumpkin or ensure that you pay close attention to the sugar or salt level.

Fish and Shellfish

Eating seafood can naturally help lower your blood sugar. Of course, these foods are low in calories, which can help you maintain a healthy body weight, manage diabetes, or prevent high blood sugar. When it comes to fish, omega-3s and fatty acids are commonly found. Salmon, for example, is abundant in vitamin D, potassium, and antioxidants. Some studies suggest that eating the right types of fish can assist not only in lowering blood sugar naturally but also in lowering triglycerides and inflammation. If you are diabetic or have pre-diabetes, fish is a fantastic choice.

Nuts and Seeds

Nuts and seeds that naturally lower blood sugar include almonds, walnuts, pistachios, chia seeds, and flax seeds. They are high in protein and fiber. They are low in calories, yet they can fill you up and give you early satiety (meaning you feel full quickly).

You will have less room to eat fatty or unhealthy foods after consuming these low-calorie foods. A study found that eating walnuts may be beneficial in lowering blood sugar levels. They discovered that patients who ate walnuts, which contain antioxidants, could reduce their chance of getting type 2 diabetes by up to half in certain cases. Another benefit of nuts and seeds is that certain studies have shown that they boost insulin sensitivity and lower blood sugar levels.

Lentils and Beans

This food has a high protein and fiber content, making them a healthy 2-for-1 nutritional component to every meal yet is low in calories. Lentils and beans can naturally reduce blood sugar. They can also assist in naturally reducing cholesterol and unblocking your arteries. With so many different types of beans available, there's likely to be one that appeals to you.

Because of their high protein content, beans are an excellent meat substitute. Beans, unlike meat, contain no saturated fat and plenty of fiber, making them a healthy alternative.

Beans are usually grouped with carbs such as bread and potatoes when looking at exchange lists. But keep in mind that beans are substantially higher in protein and fiber than other starchy foods. Beans also include a considerable amount of soluble fiber, which feeds healthy gut bacteria and has been shown in animal studies to promote gut health and lower insulin resistance. More study in humans is required, although the present findings are encouraging.

While beans may seem a little bland at first, be careful not to add too much salt or to cook baked beans with pork fat. Diabetes increases your chances of having heart problems. Don't ruin the health benefits of beans by adding too much salt or salty foods. Instead, try other spices like cumin, garlic, and sage.

Beans are not only a healthy supplement to your diet, but they are also easily preserved and affordable. Canned beans have a lengthy shelf life, making them a perfect pantry staple for an easy-to-use, low-glycemic food.

Sauerkraut

Who would have thought that eating sauerkraut would help to naturally lower blood sugar? Sauerkraut is a German word that means "sour cabbage." It's a traditional German food made with fermented cabbage. The fermenting process helps to keep microorganisms off the sauerkraut, allowing it to be stored for longer than normal cabbage. It offers many of the same health advantages as regular fresh cabbage, plus some additional benefits from the fermentation. You get some probiotics from the sauerkraut, which helps with digestion.

If you take a serving of half a cup of sauerkraut (just 16 calories), it is a low-calorie food. It has no carbohydrates, cholesterol, or sugar, and it's high in fiber, with 2g of fiber per serving, which we know is another natural approach to reducing blood sugar. Before eating sauerkraut, be aware that it can contain a lot of sodium. One serving of sauerkraut has 219 mg of salt, and we all know that if you want to be healthy and have good blood pressure, you should eat a low-salt diet. What does that suggest? Yes, sauerkraut is another way to lower blood sugar naturally, but take it in moderation and use caution if you can't handle high sodium levels in your diet.

CARB-FRIENDLY STRATEGIES

These helpful strategies will help you avoid blood sugar spike without sacrificing carbs.

Rice, pasta, bread, and potatoes are all inexpensive, convenient comfort foods that form the foundation of most people's diets, but there is concern that eating these high-carb foods may cause blood sugar levels to spike, sending your blood sugar levels on a roller coaster ride all day is almost certainly not ideal for your long-term health.

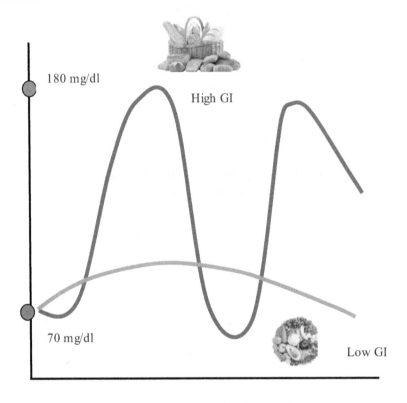

180 mg/dl

High GI

70 mg/dl

Low GI

Normal blood sugar at 70mg/dl

Blood sugar spike at 180mg/dl

Below are the best methods to avoid blood sugar spikes without limiting carbohydrate intake: To begin with, let us define a blood sugar spike. A blood sugar spike refers to a rise in blood sugar levels of 180 mg/dl or higher. Considering there is evidence that high blood sugar levels, even consistent spikes, are linked to detrimental health effects, it is ideal for us to prevent these spikes and maintain an average blood sugar level between 70 to 140 mg/dl. There was also research that young healthy and lean people with excellent glucose tolerance may never experience such blood sugar spikes no matter what they eat, but if you have diabetes, you will. The good news is that you can generally avoid blood sugar spikes and you don't need to restrict your carbohydrate consumption to do so. I don't mean to scare you but my intention is to give you the knowledge and tools required to maintain the lowest possible average blood sugar levels while averting spikes. Take, for example, a 51-year-old woman with HbA1c of 4.8%, which is equivalent to an average blood sugar of 91mg/dl and reflected in data from the continuous glucose monitor she has been wearing for the last two to three months unless she is experimenting wildly with other activities.

Her blood sugar levels are consistently between 80 and 140mg/dl, with most of the time falling below 120mg per deciliter. How will she go about it? Should she go on a low-carbohydrate diet?

(No, she prefers to eat a lot of fruits, bread, rice, potatoes, and starchy veggies)

Here's the thing; there are a few crucial things she can pay attention to so that all of those high glycemic index foods don't put her blood sugar on a wild roller coaster trip. Let's look at the following evidence-based approaches for preventing high blood sugar spikes:

i. Eat Less High-Glycemic Foods

The glycemic index is a metric used to describe how the body responds to 50g of carbs that are readily available. The glycemic index tells us that eating foods with a high glycemic index, such as white rice, cornflakes white flour bread, potato soda, or beer, causes an increase in blood sugar. It's similar to consuming pure sugar. If the majority of your meals throughout the day consist of high glycemic index foods, such as cornflakes with milk for breakfast, a sandwich made from white wheat bread for lunch, and white rice or boiled potatoes for dinner, your blood sugar curve throughout the day might look like a roller coaster, so avoiding such foods with a high glycemic index of more than about 60 is a good first step to lowering blood sugar responses after a meal. To give you an example, if you replace the cornflakes with a porridge made from steel kettles, use sourdough rye bread instead of white wheat bread to make your sandwich for lunch, and a boiled sweet potato for dinner instead of white rice or white potatoes, you could easily lower your blood sugar levels throughout the day by 20 to 30 percent without reducing your total carbohydrate intake. I'm not too devoted about this, but whenever you consume food with a high glycemic index, it's very crucial to employ one of the other approaches outlined later in this discussion to keep blood sugar levels from increasing excessively.

ii. Eat Starchy Foods After They Have Undergone Retrogradation

This means that when you cook and eat starchy foods like potatoes or rice immediately, practically all of the starch is readily broken down to glucose by your digestive enzymes and all of the glucose enters the bloodstream fast, which is why these foods cause such a spike in blood sugar. However, if you cook rice, potatoes, or any other starchy food and then cool them overnight, preferably in the fridge, some of the starch will adopt a different structure, becoming what we call resistant starch. Because this starch is now resistant to digestion and cannot be broken down by your digestive enzymes, it is referred to as resistant starch. Additionally, the glucose is kind of enveloped in the starch and cannot be absorbed into your bloodstream. This may have some extra benefits, but the key point here is that starchy foods that passed through this retrogradation process and hence contain some resistant starch raised blood sugar levels far less than starch that had not undergone retrogradation. The glycemic index of cooked and cooled starchy foods can be 20 to 40% lower than that of the same food eaten straight. After cooking, you quickly realize that this is a strategy that with some planning, you can use with ease. For example, when you cook potatoes, you can always make a few extra, store them in the fridge overnight, and then use them the next day to make potato salad or hash browns. The same goes for rice, which may be used for stir fry the next day.

iii. Don't Eat Naked Carbs

Carbs are considered naked if they are consumed without much protein, fat, or fiber. For example, cornflakes with milk, instant oatmeal with jam, white bread with jam, or risotto may have a trace of protein, fat, or fiber, but the meal is virtually entirely composed of readily digestible carbohydrates or sugar. Numerous studies have demonstrated clearly that adding protein to a meal high in carbohydrates significantly lowers the blood sugar response. To some extent, adding some fat or fiber from foods such as vegetables may also help. Based on scientific research, it is recommended for you to consider adding a protein source to a meal that contains high-carbohydrate foods such as bread, pasta, rice, oats, corn flakes, etc. The higher the glycemic index of the food, the more crucial it is to include some protein; meat, fish or shellfish, eggs, Greek yogurt, beans, lentils, or tofu. Although some of them also contain fat as well, but you should also think about getting fat from nuts and seeds, avocados, olives or using a small amount of olive oil.

Combining foods high on the glycemic index with leafy greens like spinach and lettuce; cruciferous vegetables like broccoli, cabbage, cauliflower, and Brussels sprouts; and non-starchy veggies like onions, leeks, fennel, and celery is also a smart option. Your blood sugar spike will be lowered if you combine protein, fat, and fiber-rich vegetables with high-carb foods in one meal. It's possible that you've heard the advice to eat foods high in carbohydrates last and those robust in protein and fiber first. True, this may drop blood sugar response even more than consuming all of the foods at once. Most of the time, I think this is impractical, and the extra benefit is probably not that great—take, for instance, a high glycemic index breakfast of white bread and jam. Now, my suggestion would be for you to eat something else for breakfast because, aside from its high glycemic index, this food is not particularly nutritious, but let's ignore that for the time being. Let's say you're craving a delicious Sunday morning breakfast of bread and coffee. Your blood sugar response will likely be halved if you simply add a few scrambled or boiled eggs to this meal, or substitute the white bread for whole grain sourdough rye bread with peanut butter or cheese and maybe even still include an egg or two. Let's look at an example from a dinner I had with some friends where we had a traditional German cuisine of mashed potatoes, sauerkraut, and some kind of smoked pork. Mashed potatoes have a high glycemic index, but this complex meal contains a reasonable amount of protein, fat, and a large serving of a non-starchy vegetable. What do you think my blood response would be?

My blood sugar response, based on the example, will be fairly low and peak around 120 mg per deciliter. The essential takeaway from this example is to avoid eating naked carbs, especially if a typical serving of your meal has a glycemic load of 10 or higher. Try combining it with some fat, protein, and a sizeable portion of non-starchy vegetables. Also, consider portion sizes when you are fixing a plate for yourself.

iv. Add Vinegar to High-Carb Meals

There are a lot of studies that show that having vinegar with or before high-carb meals will significantly lessen your blood sugar response. Vinegar, even when diluted, is a strong acid. I don't enjoy it and wouldn't drink it daily, but even if you do, drinking it might negatively impact your dental health or mucous membranes in your oral cavity, esophagus, or stomach in the long run. My advice is to do what many cultures do: have a little salad with vinaigrette before or with a high-carb meal, or have pickles with your sandwich. If you love it, you'll be more likely to make it part of your regular routine and the salad or pickled vegetables you'll be eating with the vinegar will probably provide you with some extra benefits.

You can use apple cider vinegar (which is what most research studies use), but any vinegar will work just fine. It probably doesn't matter if you take the vinegar with or before your high-carb meal. Let me give you a practical example, say I had leftover mashed potatoes with caramelized onions and sauerkraut for lunch, what should I do? I'll definitely have a small salad with vinaigrette before eating the mashed potatoes and sauerkraut. The blood sugar response will be minimal here as well. There are at least three possible explanations for why my blood sugar won't rise by more than 20mg per deciliter. The first reason is that the salad, which included vinegar, may have helped, secondly, it is also possible that the sauerkraut helped also, and thirdly, the mashed potatoes that had been refrigerated overnight, causing some of the starch to convert to resistant starch (keep in mind that strategy number two, "retrogradation").

v. Take Advantage of the Second Meal Effect

The second meal effect happens when what we eat for breakfast impacts our blood sugar response to our lunch or when our blood sugar response to our dinner is influenced by what we eat for lunch. The most crucial research finding worth knowing is that the carbs you eat at one meal actually lower your blood sugar response at the next meal. Consider the following scenario: A lady eats a specific high-carb meal consisting of rice and veggies two days in a row.

She had a high-carb lunch on the first day, which includes tuna and potatoes. The second meal effect will forecast how her blood sugar responds if she has a lunch (such as a steak with butter and a salad with olive oil) that is low-carb the next day. One way to think about it is that when you eat carbohydrates, your body prepares to tolerate additional carbohydrates, or vice versa. If you don't eat carbs, even for one meal, your body's ability to handle carbs declines slightly. This means that if you decide to follow a low-carb diet, you should eat, educate yourself about the various types of carbohydrates, know about all the meals you eat, know about the carb counts and serving sizes of the foods you eat, and avoid alternating between meals that are high-carb and low-carb all the time.

Another aspect of the second meal effect is that if one meal is high in protein or fiber, it lowers the blood sugar response at the next meal. So, if you eat a high protein, high fiber breakfast, you will help keep your blood sugar response low both at breakfast and at the subsequent lunch altogether. The second meal effect is a further reason why we should limit our intake of high-glycemic index foods like white rice, potatoes, and baked goods and instead include protein and some fiber source, like non-starchy vegetables, in every meal.

The hormone insulin aids in blood sugar regulation by removing glucose from the bloodstream after a meal. Recall that the hormone insulin is released in greater amounts when blood sugar levels rise following a meal. Insulin does many things, but in the muscle, it attaches to the insulin receptor, causing a shift inside the cell that allows glucose transporters, glut4 to be transported to the cell membrane; glucose can then enter the muscle cells from the blood, and blood sugar levels lower.

This may not function perfectly in insulin-resistant people. So, here's the good news: muscle cells can absorb glucose from the blood without the use of insulin. Imagine if muscle cells could only take up sugar from the blood after a meal and only with the help of insulin. Our species would have died ago since we wouldn't have had time to unwrap that sandwich and take a bite when the saber-tooth tiger attacked. So, in short, muscle cells that are being exercised take up glucose from the blood in a way that is completely independent of insulin, and it's not surprising that there is a lot of scientific evidence showing that any muscle contraction after a meal will significantly reduce the increase in blood sugar levels. The research suggests that exercise should begin within 30 minutes of finishing a meal. Most people probably don't want to exercise vigorously after a meal, but even a 10- or 15-minute walk around the block is better than nothing, especially after having large meals high in glycemic index. I'd say the longer the better. To demonstrate the impact of walking on blood sugar levels, consider two situations involving a woman with celiac disease. During the Christmas break, she paid a visit to her relatives, who had already prepared a gluten-free coffee cake for all of their visitors. Because her relatives thought the entire cake was not enough for her, they brought several packages of gluten-free Christmas cookies specifically for her. So, when the coffee cake and cookies arrived, she ate four slices of cake and about 20 cookies, which she munched on for almost an hour.

Still, it's quite clear what happens to her blood sugar. Predictably, a blood sugar spike of up to 190mg/dl. It's a little absurd to consume this much refined flour and sugar in one sitting. So, she did it again the next day, but this time she had a hard-boiled egg a few minutes before she started the cake and cookies feast, followed by a 60-minute walk, her blood sugar level looked like well, there was still an increase to about 140mg/dl, but that increase is 50mg/dl less pronounced than the day before; 50mg/dl less from having a pretty substantial blood sugar spike. Despite the massive amount of cake and cookies, her blood sugar remained in the normal homeostatic range of 70 to 140mg/dl.

It wasn't just the walk, but also some protein from the egg. So, let's look at what the walk does: Ms. Jada, for example, was on a trip that included a four-hour car ride. She ate some bread and potato chips while driving (keep in mind, she wasn't moving the entire time because she was driving). Her blood sugar level rose to 170mg/dl as a result. The mistake she made was eating something with a high glycemic index when she knew she wouldn't be able to move for four hours afterward. Picture another scenario where she eats the same bread and potato chips but then goes for a stroll. Assuming that the meal began at 1:50 p.m., when do you think she stopped walking? Let's say she got home at 2:45 p.m. and cooled off. Even after eating so much, she still had a lot of glucose entering her blood, and her blood sugar levels increased to about 150 mg/dl. While this was an improvement over earlier, it would have been preferable in this instance if she had walked for at least 30 minutes or more.

These strategies are based on scientific research about the blood sugar response to carbs, but they may not be enough to get your blood sugar levels back into normal range. If you have frequent blood sugar rises, you are probably glucose intolerant to some extent. At the very least, to fully normalize your blood sugar levels, you must also improve your glucose tolerance. For example, if you have diabetes and have an HbA1c of 7.5, your average blood sugar level is around 170mg/dl and your fasting blood sugar level is around 130mg/dl.

Your blood sugar will probably spike to more than 200 mg/dl after every meal if you are not mindful. This will probably happen if you do not use any of the above-discussed strategies, which include eating naked high-glycemic index carbohydrates with every meal, not moving around after a large meal, not eating any salad or vegetables, etc.

You may almost certainly avoid these spikes and lower your HbA1c to, say, 6% by using these six scientifically proven methods. That's an improvement than before, but your blood sugar levels are still too high, and you still have diabetes. To drop your blood sugar levels more optimally into the non-diabetic range, you must improve your glucose tolerance, which is your body's inherent ability to manage blood sugar levels in a normal range.

PREVENTING PREDIABETES PROGRESSION

With these actionable prevention strategies, you can prevent prediabetes from progressing to diabetes.

Strategies to Reverse Prediabetes Naturally & Lower Blood Sugar Without Medication

If you're on the edge of needing blood sugar medication or wish to lower your A1c, keep reading. We will go over 5 natural ways to reverse prediabetes without using medication.

Tip #1: Know Your Numbers

It's critical that you know your numbers. But I strongly advise you to comprehend your numbers and determine whether you are in the healthy range of pre-diabetes or diabetes. Then, repeat the test as frequently as your doctor advises, or at the very least, every six to 12 months, to track your progress over time.

Here's a quick rundown of fasting blood sugar and A1c. If you have never had your fasting blood sugar tested, you should consider doing a water fast, which is going 8–12 hours without eating and only drinking water before your blood is collected for test. This can be done in the doctor's office, but if you want to monitor your blood sugar and ketone levels at home, I suggest using the Keto Mojo device. It is a quick, painless finger prick that provides a reading in a matter of seconds.

Your hemoglobin A1c is not the same as your fasting blood sugar. The A1C test determines how much of your hemoglobin (a protein in red blood cells that transports oxygen) is coated with sugar.

This test is often employed to diagnose diabetes and assess a patient's level of diabetic management. The higher your A1C score, the worse your blood sugar control and the greater your risk of diabetes complications.

Let's take a look at the normal, prediabetic, and diabetic ranges for fasting blood sugar and hemoglobin A1c.

	Fasting Blood Sugar	HbA1c
Normal	Between 70-100, although closer to 70 is better.	5.7%
Prediabetes	Between 100-125.	5.7 to 6.4%,
Type 2 diabetes	2 separate readings of 126 or higher.	6.5% and higher.

These values are intriguing because they connect your A1c to your average blood glucose levels. For example, if your A1c is 9%, your average blood glucose should be approximately 212.

So, why do we care so much about fasting blood glucose and A1c levels? Both of these are crucial indicators of the underlying condition known as insulin resistance. However, if you have high blood glucose for an extended period, your insulin may struggle to keep up, requiring more and more insulin. It's a vicious cycle that leads to insulin resistance which is linked to a variety of health problems, including obesity, heart disease, diabetes, and dementia. Lower your blood sugars if you want to lower your insulin. According to one study, insulin is reduced when blood sugars fall below roughly 83, so while up to 99 is deemed "normal," it's clearly not optimal.

It's time to take action after you've checked your fasting blood sugar and/or HbA1c levels. Don't put off getting your blood sugar tested; it can be eye-opening and empowering to witness the improvements on the inside even if your weight loss is slow on the outside.

Tip #2: Factors that Influence Blood Sugar and Insulin Levels

You must educate yourself about the various kinds of macronutrients and how they influence your blood sugar levels. Change your focus from counting calories or points to counting macros instead; they are more significant, and we measure what matters. Macronutrients are classified into three main categories: carbs, protein, and fat.

Fiber, starch, and sugar are all carbs. Refined starches and sugars are those that have been processed to remove all of the protein and fat, leaving only carbohydrates. Refined and processed carbs and sugars will cause the highest blood sugar and thus insulin spike, thus you should limit your intake of these.

Fiber, on the other hand, has a reverse effect, slowing digestion and preventing sugar spikes. Whole-food carbohydrate sources with a high fiber content are therefore beneficial to your health. I'm referring to foods such as non-starchy veggies, avocados, olives, blackberries, and raspberries, among others.

Protein has little effect on blood sugar levels, although it does elevate blood insulin somewhat, while dietary fat has the least effect on blood sugar and insulin response. It's much easier to make good food choices if you've established an overall framework for how food affects insulin.

Tip #3: Stress

You might be shocked to learn that trimming down and preventing diseases isn't all about food. It's all about hormones, specifically insulin. Cortisol, your stress hormone, also influences insulin. When we are stressed, particularly chronic stress, our cortisol levels rise. As a reminder, sleep deprivation is a sort of stress on your body. Multiple studies have found a link between sleep deprivation and diabetes. According to one study, men who reported difficulty sleeping were nearly 5 times more likely to acquire diabetes, while those who reported sleeping for a shorter period were nearly 3 times more likely. Because our bodies are built to resist or flee from stress, as cortisol levels rise, blood sugar levels rise as well. To do so, our muscles require energy, thus blood sugar is released in anticipation of the requirement for energy to fight or flee.

However, if our stress is mental or emotional, and we do not need to use our muscles, that blood sugar is not burned up, thus extra insulin is required to push it into the cells. That is how blood sugar enters your cells; it is either pushed in by insulin or pulled in by muscle demand.

Tip #4: Move Your Body

Going for a short walk after dinner might be quite beneficial for decreasing your blood glucose after a high-carb meal. As previously stated, there are two basic ways for glucose to leave your bloodstream: insulin pushes or muscle pulls. Exercise, or simply moving around, can help you lower your blood sugar levels. The glut4 transporter is responsible for transporting blood sugar from the circulation to the cells. Going for a walk not only helps to lower your immediate blood sugar but also minimizes the amount of insulin necessary to process the carbs you just ate. The ideal type of workout is one that you will really do, however, I believe strength training exercises are more beneficial. Muscle mass is essential to retain as you age to keep your metabolism going and to be able to function normally and freely. For all major muscle groups, I recommend strength training at a moderate to high intensity twice a week.

Intermittent fasting is a revolutionary lifestyle that is completely free and calls for less cooking and dishes, which I always enjoy. When you don't eat, your body is forced to use fuel that is already accessible. It begins with the glucose that is already circulating in your blood from your previous meal, then moves into your short-term stored glucose in the form of glycogen, and finally taps into your body fat. Again, weight loss is about hormones, not calories. There are various hormonal benefits to intermittent fasting that chronic calorie restriction does not provide. Restricting some foods all of the time is not the same as restricting all foods some of the time.

Tip #6: Consume Fermented Foods or Beverages

Apple cider vinegar is my favorite. There are two major advantages to eating fermented foods. The first is that when the bacteria ferment the food, they are eating through the starches or sugars rather than the protein and fat, so they are essentially digesting some of the carb digestion for us. The bacteria we consume by ingesting fermented food or liquid foods means we get less starch than the non-fermented version. Another advantage of beneficial gut bacteria is that they can act as probiotics in our intestines. Several studies have demonstrated that consuming one to two tablespoons of apple cider vinegar with a starchy meal reduces the glucose and insulin effect of that meal in insulin-resistant people and may assist in improving glucose management in people with type 2 diabetes in general. A study also discovered that ingesting two tablespoons of raw apple cider vinegar in the evening helped manage glucose levels the next morning, reducing the normal dawn effect of raised blood sugars caused by the morning rush of cortisol. You could start with one to two tablespoons of apple cider vinegar in the morning and evening. If you wish to make the taste satisfactory, dilute it with some water.

Tip #7: Don't Skip Breakfast

It is well acknowledged that breakfast is the most significant meal of the day, and this may be particularly true for those who have type 2 diabetes. In one small case, for example, researchers examined the food intake and blood sugar levels of 22 persons with type 2 diabetes for two days. The only difference between the two days' food consumption was that the participants ate breakfast one morning but not the following. The study found that for those who skipped breakfast, their blood sugar levels were higher all day. According to studies, skipping breakfast may impair the function of the pancreas's beta cells, which produce insulin.

But keep in mind that any breakfast won't serve to keep your blood sugar levels stable. Breakfast choices are crucial. I urge people to consider alternatives to the typical cereal box. Sugary cereal accompanied by a large glass of juice is not healthy. For a diabetic-friendly breakfast, I suggest going for nutritious, well-balanced options like scrambled eggs with tomatoes, mushrooms, and spinach.

It has long been known that gum disease can result from type 2 diabetes. However, according to studies, having unhealthy gums may raise blood sugar levels in the body (American Dental Association, ADA). Gum disease can raise the body's susceptibility to infections and inflammation, both of which can raise blood sugar levels.

The ADA recommends that individuals with type 2 diabetes take additional care of their gums. Brush and floss twice a day, and schedule routine check-ups with your dentist to have your gums examined. Ensure that your dentist knows about your diabetes.

Picking Your Fats Wisely

The good news is that a nutritious diet can help you lower your blood sugar levels. Foods high in healthy fat and protein are satiating, which means they keep you full from one meal to the next. They are also nutrient-dense (unlike carbohydrates, which are typically stored as energy). Whole milk creamer, half-and-half string cheese, full-fat Greek yogurt, cottage cheese, and butter or ghee are all excellent sources of fat from dairy.

Saturated fat is one of the few nutrients that has been shown to raise HDL (high-density lipoprotein) cholesterol, which is protective against heart disease. Overall, saturated fats do not harm blood profiles as previously believed, so if you're worried about eating a lot of it because you're afraid of having high cholesterol, you don't have to be. Because fatty fish are abundant in omega-3 fatty acids, notably EPA (eicosapentaenoic acid) and DHA (docosahexaenoic acid), which are anti-inflammatory, it is another excellent high-fat food that would help maintain insulin and keep sugar levels low. Plant sources of omega-3s, such as walnuts, chia seeds, and flax seeds, have more ALA (alpha-lipoic acid). Because the conversion rate of ALA to EPA and DHA is only approximately 8 to 15%, if you want the anti-inflammatory effects of omega-3s, you'll need to receive the EPA and DHA from fatty fish like tuna, trout, salmon, herring, mackerel, cod, and the likes. If you don't want to consume fish, you can get it from algae oil, but make sure to see your doctor before taking any supplements.

Omega-6 fatty acids are found in nuts and seeds and are healthy, just like any other medication, but omega-6 fatty acids contained in refined oils from those nuts and seeds are not healthy, this is a huge difference. While whole-food omega-6 is excellent, processed omega-6 is inflammatory, even if it does not directly elevate blood sugar or insulin levels. Healthy fats, such as omega-9 fatty acids or monounsaturated fats found in whole foods such as avocados, olives, nuts, and seeds, are beneficial to your health and can help maintain blood sugar and keep insulin levels low.

In addition to the processed omega-6 fatty acid oil another unhealthy fat to avoid is artificial trans fats and foods containing them.

There are some naturally occurring trans fats in animals that are not harmful. The words "Partially hydrogenated Oils" should also be avoided because they contain trans fats. The Food and Drug Administration (FDA) stated in 2015 that partially hydrogenated oil is no longer generally recognized as safe (GRAS). They said that removing it from food may save thousands of lives each year, and the FDA went even further in 2018, banning trans fats from new food products.

Palm oil and palm kernel oil are becoming more popular in food products; they are heavy in saturated fatty acids (approximately 50 and 80 percent, respectively), with the remaining part being unsaturated fats.

The smoke points of different oils should also be taken into account. This chart below will assist you in reviewing common oil smoke points.

HIGH HEAT OIL

Stir-frying, Frying,
Grilling, Broiling, Sautéing

480-520°F	Refined Avocado Oil
450-500°F	Safflower Oil
400-475°F	Canola Oil
450°F	Soybean Oil
450°F	Refined Sunflower Oil
450°F	Refined Peanut Oil
400-450°F	Refined Coconut Oil

MEDIUM HEAT OIL

Sautéing, Baking, Roasting
Veggies, Searing Meat

425°F	Hazelnut Oil
390-420°F	Grapeseed Oil
410°F	Refined Sesame Oil
400°F	Macadamia Oil
325-400°F	Unrefined Extra Virgin Olive Oil
350-400°F	Unrefined Avocado Oil
400°F	Vegetable Oil

LOW HEAT OIL

Sautéing, Sauces,
Caramelizing Veggies

350-380°F	Unrefined Coconut oil
350°F	Unrefined Sesame oil
320°F	Unrefined Sunflower oil
320°F	Unrefined Peanut oil
320°F	Unrefined Walnut oil
300-330°F	Hemp Seed oil

NO HEAT OIL

Garnishing, Dips, Salad
Dressing

225°F	Unrefined Almond Oil
225°F	Unrefined Flax seed Oil

Smoking is an indication that your oil is breaking down; breaking down in oils can release compounds that cause food to taste burnt or bitter, or they can cause inflammation, which can be harmful to the body. Before using any oil, ensure its smoke point is appropriate for the cooking method you intend to use. For example, if you normally prepare homemade chicken nuggets with a butter-dark-olive-oil combo, you can simply use butter instead of the oxidized olive oil. When frying or cooking at high temperatures, consider using fats such as clarified butter, light olive oil, or beef tallow.

WEIGHT LOSS WITH INSULIN RESISTANCE

Discover how to lower blood sugar and lose weight with insulin resistance.

What if I told you that the diabetic plate method advised by the American Diabetes Association is not the best strategy to reverse pre-diabetes or diabetes? Hopefully, this discussion will help you understand why and how to eat the best foods to lower blood sugar and blood insulin. If you're one of the estimated 88% of adults who have insulin resistance, these are also the best foods to help you lose weight with insulin resistance. Insulin resistance raises the risk of a variety of comorbidities, including obesity, diabetes, heart disease, and dementia among others. Making healthy food choices to lower blood sugar becomes straightforward once you understand how different macronutrients affect your blood sugar and insulin. If you have a direct family member who has diabetes, your risk is increased, but you are not predestined to develop the disease; genetics certainly play a role, but lifestyle is more important. Carbophobia is another barrier people face while learning how to diet to lower blood sugar. They get reluctant to eat any carbs and wind up on an unsustainable restrictive diet. Not all carbs are bad for you, and as we've previously discussed and will continue to do so, you'll learn which ones to eat and which to avoid.

One important point to remember is that if you have pre-diabetes or diabetes, you have insulin resistance. Insulin resistance is what is causing your high blood sugars, and if you truly want to improve your health, you must learn how to live a low-insulin lifestyle; in fact, fasting insulin can predict type 2 diabetes up to two decades before fasting blood sugar. The sooner you take control of your blood sugar, the better. If you're already trying to eat a lower-sugar diet, we will be uncovering some sugar-free ingredients that are sitting in plain sight yet nevertheless raise your blood sugar levels. I urge you to ponder on the following question: What is the simplest thing I can change that will have the greatest influence on my health? Start there and work your way up. It could be as simple as switching from white or whole wheat pasta to pasta made from edamame or chickpeas; simple and quick is how healthy habits are formed. What is the rationale for a normal glucose level? Let's say when you have your fasting blood glucose done it is 126 or above on two separate tests, you have an A1c of 6.5 or higher, what do you do then?

What About Prediabetes?

To begin, let's define pre-diabetes and discuss the various testing for pre-diabetes. Let's consider the scenario of Jada, a lady who tracks her food consumption but not her blood glucose levels because her doctor told her it didn't matter because her A1c was less than 7. However, in the last 3-4 months, she decided to check her daily fasting glucose level. When Jada checked one morning, she discovered that she was getting values ranging from 140 to 165 and that it occasionally went up to 190. Jada had an A1c of 5.9 at her most recent checkup. What do you think happened with Jada's numbers? What actions do you believe she ought to take? In a nutshell, Jada lost a little weight by tracking her calories, but she wasn't sure what to do next. Was this to truly optimize her blood sugars and maintain her weight loss? Let's answer the questions.

Recall that when her A1c was less than 7, her doctor advised her not to worry about it, but now it is above the 6.5 range close to 7. As we previously learned, that is a point around the diabetic cutoff, but her doctor advised her not to worry about it, and now she is diabetic. My expectation is that at that point when she wasn't close to the diabetic range, the doctor would take action by writing a prescription, but there are a lot of proactive steps that may be taken to avoid the need for medication.

Overall, our medical system isn't well-equipped to prevent disease when you have just five to ten minutes with your doctor, they don't have time to sit down and explain to you what it takes to lower blood sugar but they do have time to write a prescription, and I know this time process frustrates doctors as well because they are totally into the profession to help people.

The oral glucose tolerance test (OGTT) which is another test that's a little more involved than the fasting blood sugar or A1c test, refers to how well your body processes glucose after being given a measured dose of usually 75g orally (75g of glucose is the equivalent amount of sugar in almost two cups of pasta or 1/3 cup of white rice). Normally, when you consume a single serving of glucose like this, your blood sugar rises and then falls over the next few hours, but if you have pre-diabetes or type 2 diabetes, your blood sugar takes more time to lower. Here are the cutoffs for the oral glucose tolerance test 2 hours after taking 75g of glucose:

- *A blood glucose level below 140mg/dl is considered normal*
- *A blood glucose level between 140 to 199mg/dl indicates pre-diabetes (sometimes referred to as impaired fasting glucose)*
- *A blood glucose level of 200mg/dl or higher indicates diabetes.*

As previously stated, fasting insulin can predict type 2 diabetes up to two decades before fasting glucose.

The kraft test is another test that can assist in tracking blood sugar and insulin-resistant levels. This test is a combined test that evaluates the body's reaction to insulin and glucose after a meal. Because it also measures the insulin in the background that is important for managing your blood glucose, the kraft test can detect pre-diabetes even before your blood glucose level rises.

High insulin levels are linked to the same conditions as type 2 diabetes, such as cardiovascular disease, osteoporosis, dementia, Inflammation, blindness, and peripheral neuropathy. Let me give a brief explanation of how the kraft test works. It is a step up from the oral glucose tolerance test and can detect pre-diabetes by looking at a person's insulin response rather than just their fasting glucose response. The kraft test involves you taking 75g of glucose and then your glucose and insulin levels are measured at the 30-minute, 1-hour, 2-hour, and 3-hour marks to make the curves during a person's examination to see the relationships between a person's glucose and insulin response; a pre-diabetic may still have a relatively normal blood glucose response.

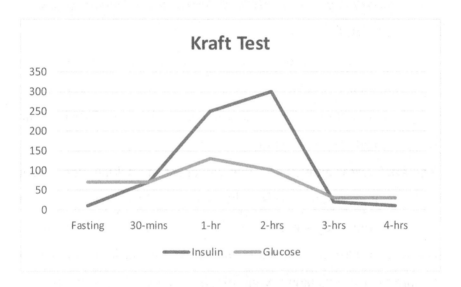

In those with a good insulin response, the insulin curve should follow the blood glucose curve, but in people with pre-diabetes, the insulin curve will be higher because more insulin will be needed. This is because the cells are less susceptible to the effects of insulin; their bodies are slightly insulin resistant, but their insulin can still keep up, lowering blood sugar levels.

However, their body will eventually be unable to produce enough insulin to keep up, and they will develop impaired fasting glucose or pre-diabetes. According to a 2017 research study, using a fasting glucose oral glucose tolerance test or a1c may not be the most effective early screening tool for type 2 diabetes. Incorporating fasting insulin, particularly insulin after an oral glucose tolerance test, as enhanced screening methods may help to increase the ability to detect diabetes and pre-diabetes, allowing for earlier intervention to prevent diabetic complications.

Most pre-diabetics also battle with weight gain or poor body composition, which implies less muscle mass and more fat mass. This is because insulin is the key hormone responsible for body weight. Increased fat mass is a direct cause of insulin resistance because insulin is the hormone responsible for its production. Then, when your insulin rises, your fat rises, and your leptin rises, you become resistant not only to insulin but also to leptin. Leptin assists in counteracting the effects of ghrelin, or your hunger hormone so that the negative feedback loop that is supposed to keep you at a healthy weight is disrupted. Leptin no longer inhibits ghrelin, causing you to feel hungry and eat even though your body has enough fat for fuel. The most effective strategy to fix this and regain healthy body fat and weight is to begin at the source, lower insulin resistance.

What Do You Know About the Symptoms

When we focus on lowering insulin, all of your other risk factor numbers improve, including triglycerides, blood pressure, HDL cholesterol, glucose, and body fat, particularly the unhealthy visceral belly fat that is inflammatory. When we look at hidden symptoms of pre-diabetes, we are really looking at hidden symptoms of insulin resistance and increased blood sugars since that is what triggers your diabetes.

Approximately 88 million adults in the United States, or more than one in three, have pre-diabetes, according to the Centers for Disease Control (CDC). More than 84 percent of persons with pre-diabetes are unaware they have it, therefore it's safe to say the most prevalent symptom of pre-diabetes is none at all or none that they identify as being related to pre-diabetes. However, weight gain, notably a gain in fat mass, is the most common symptom of pre-diabetes. As previously stated, insulin regulates not only blood sugar but also weight.

Excessive cravings, particularly for carbon sugar cravings, can be a symptom of pre-diabetes. Cells that are resistant to insulin will sense a bit of starvation and increase your hunger, especially for meals known to provide quick energy (refined carbohydrates). Another symptom of pre-diabetes is *Excessive Thirst* which can cause an increased fluid intake leading to increased urination, another sign of pre-diabetes.

Elevated Blood Pressure is a common sign of pre-diabetes; increased insulin directly causes high blood pressure. High blood pressure may be the first indicator of insulin resistance or pre-diabetes in some people; you may simply have not been aware of the connection.

Fatigue is a typical symptom of pre-diabetes, and it can be caused by a variety of factors. The blood sugar spikes and dips that follow from munching on carbs are a major cause of fatigue; your body is simply expending a lot of energy just trying to balance your blood sugars.

Other symptoms of high blood sugar include blurred vision, numbness, and tingling in your hands or feet (called peripheral neuropathy), which can be excruciatingly painful and severely limit activities. Infections are another indicator of pre-diabetes. High blood sugar hinders white blood cell function, which is essential for a healthy immune system, and sugar is an excellent source of energy for invading bacteria and fungi. All of these factors raise the likelihood of infections of all sorts and damage the immune system, making it take longer to heal. Upper respiratory infections and urinary tract infections are two of the most common types of infections. If you realize you're getting more of them, consider it a warning sign to check your blood sugar and, if necessary, get them under control. Slow-healing wounds are associated with weak immune response, which is why persons with diabetes, particularly those with peripheral neuropathy who may not be able to feel effectively, must be cautious about physically monitoring their feet for cuts and treating them very early. Diabetic foot wounds can be extremely difficult to heal, leading to amputations of toes or, in some cases, the entire foot or leg.

The final symptom we'll look at is brain fog or confusion. Your brain is also insulin sensitive; in fact, Alzheimer's disease is now known as type 3 diabetes. So, for those of you who are determined to maintain your cognitive health as you age, I hope knowing that there is a strong connection between diabetes and dementia provides you with strong persistent motivation to prioritize your health.

Also, some women are more likely to develop pre-diabetes or diabetes around menopause because estrogen levels drop, causing insulin resistance to rise. I don't say this to cause fear, but it's the fact; that the years preceding menopause are an extremely essential time in a woman's life for getting her blood sugars under control. You only have two choices: either prioritize your health now or plan for future illnesses. If you prioritize your health now, you'll be much better equipped to handle sickness in the future. Every choice you make will either improve or worsen your health.

Choose Healthy Food and Live!

It still amazes me that big food companies get away with marketing products with such high carbohydrate counts. One cup of these multi-grain Cheerios, for example, gives 21g of net carbs. Net carbs are total carbs minus fiber, given that fiber slows blood sugar response, yet six of those carbs are from added sugar. Some companies go ahead and add a red heart label on their products, claiming that it may lower the risk of heart disease.

Do you know what lowers the risk of heart disease? Real food that doesn't require a food label: the salmon swimming in the ocean or the avocado lying on the shelves of stores without a food label. If your meal comes out of a bag, or box or has a barcode, you should halt and look at the ingredients. If you can't pronounce them or have no idea what the food looks like, maybe it's beans or nuts, you can bet it's full of additives. By monitoring the amounts of macronutrients and the relative benefits of various foods, you can observe what you're consuming and ignore the packaging.

I also consider goods with high sugar amounts to be unhealthy, such as high-sugar fruits, candy, donuts, cake, cookies, ice cream, brownies pop, sweetened iced tea, many sports drinks or coffee beverages, and some of those good kombucha drinks. Again, there are healthy delicious alternatives to all of them that won't cause such a blood sugar surge. You really need to look out for the sugar in your drinks. Take a 12-ounce tall Starbucks large white chocolate mocha, for instance. It has 40g of sugar, which is about equivalent to the amount of added sugar in a can of Pepsi. Sugar can also be found in drink additives like coffee creamer.

Artificial Sugars and Blood Spike

Another consideration is that a food may contain no carbohydrates, it could have no calories and still affect blood sugar; this is where screening packaged foods comes in handy. The main artificial sweeteners and texture additives to avoid on the ingredients list include maltodextrin, sucralose, saccharin, aspartame, and acesulfame potassium. If it contains them, avoid it because the sugar-free product will very certainly spike your blood sugar. The first item on our list, maltodextrin, is a white powder produced from corn, rice, potato starch, or wheat. Although it is made from plants, it is extensively processed. They are added to processed foods as a thickener or filler to boost their volume, and they are also applied to personal care products like lotions and hair care. So, if eating lotion or hair care products seems appealing, go ahead and consume that maltodextrin. It serves as a preservative as well, increasing the shelf life of packaged products. It's affordable and simple to make. Additionally, maltodextrin can be used to thicken products like salad dressings, gelatin sauces, and instant pudding. Maltodextrin has a higher glycemic index than table sugar, which means it can induce a major rise or spike in your blood sugar instantly after eating foods containing it.

Artificial sweeteners; saccharin, also known as sweet and low sucralose, also known as Splenda, aspartame, NutraSweet, and acesulfame potassium, commonly known as ace-k. All of them have been shown to elevate blood sugar levels by drastically altering the makeup of your gut bacteria. Unlike maltodextrin, these are known to have post-oral metabolic effects, they may not have an immediate effect on your blood glucose, but they will contribute to insulin resistance and poor blood sugar control over time. If you're trying to cut back on sugar but still want a healthy sweetener, I recommend stevia, monk fruit, or erythritol. Stevia and monk fruit are gentler on the stomach and produce less gas than erythritol, so instead of buying a no sugar added cocoa with maltodextrin, acesulfame potassium, and sucralose, you could prepare your own with milk, cocoa powder, and stevia drops. It's simple, easy, and delicious, and it'll boost your lifestyle.

Section II

DIABETES DIET PLAN

Discover the best ways to plan your meal and lose weight with less efforts

A thoughtful diabetes diet is similar to the healthy eating plan that doctors recommend for everyone: It consists of whole, minimally processed foods that are high in fiber, as well as fiber-rich fruits and vegetables, complex carbs in moderation, lean protein, and healthy fats. It also restricts the consumption of added sugars and refined grains. There is no diabetic diet; the guidelines for healthy nutrition apply to everyone, diabetic or not. Work with your doctor and other healthcare professionals to find the most appropriate macronutrient ratio and eating plan for your health risks and goals.

The Diabetic Plate Method

Without the need to measure, calculate, or count carbs, the diabetic plate method offers a simple way to think about and prepare meals that are balanced and friendly to people with diabetes. A standard 9-inch plate is divided into three portions using the plate method. Half of your plate should be non-starchy veggies, one-quarter should be protein meals, and the remaining quarter should be carbohydrate foods like whole grains and fruits.

Non-Starchy Vegetables Can Make Up Half of Your Plate and Include Foods Such As:

- *Broccoli*
- *Spinach*
- *Kale*
- *Green Beans*
- *Mixed Salad Greens*

- *Carrots*
- *Squash*
- *Cauliflower*
- *Zucchini*
- *Cabbage*
- *Okra*
- *Tomatoes*
- *Asparagus*
- *Brussels Sprouts*
- *Mushrooms*
- *Cucumbers*

The Quarter Containing Protein Foods May Include:

- *Lean Poultry or Meat*
- *Fish Or Seafood*
- *Eggs*
- *Cheese*
- *Plant-Based Protein Foods, Like Black Beans, Kidney Beans, Pinto Beans, Lentils, Nuts and Nut Kinds of Butter, Tofu, Edamame (Soybeans), or Hummus*

The Quarter of Your Plate Filled with Carbohydrate Foods Could Include:

- *Whole Grains*
- *Whole Grain Foods, Like Whole Grain Bread and Pasta*
- *Starchy Vegetables, Like Potatoes*

- *Fruit*
- *Yogurt*
- *Milk*

These foods have the most impact on your blood sugar. You can better control your blood sugar by limiting the amount of these higher-carb foods on your plate to one-quarter of it.

Healthy fats like polyunsaturated and monounsaturated fats can be included in your diet for flavor, satiety, and—most importantly—heart health, but they don't have a set spot on your plate.

After eating, drink water or a calorie-free beverage such as a diet beverage, sparkling or infused water, or unsweetened tea.

Vegan And Vegetarian Diets

Some diabetics follow a vegetarian or vegan diet. A 2019 review found that these diets might aid in lowering waist circumference, fasting glucose, and weight. Vegetarian diets often refer to diets in which you do not eat meat but do consume animal products such as milk, eggs, and butter. Vegans do not consume any animal products, including honey, milk, and gelatin.

Diabetes-friendly vegetarian and vegan foods include:

- *Beans*
- *Soy*
- *Dark, Leafy Vegetables*
- *Nuts*
- *Legumes*

- *Fruits*
- *Whole Grains*

Vegetarian and vegan diets can be beneficial, but it's crucial to properly plan them to ensure you don't miss out on any essential nutrients.

Supplements may be necessary for vegetarians and vegans to get certain nutrients, such as:

Calcium: Found primarily in animal products such as dairy, calcium is a vital nutrient that contributes to bone and tooth health. Calcium can be obtained from broccoli and kale; however, supplements may be recommended on a vegan diet. This nutrient is also available in enriched soy milk.

Iodine: Iodine is primarily found in seafood and is required for the breakdown of food into energy. Vegetarians and vegans may struggle to meet their iodine requirements if they do not consume these animal products. Most of the required iodine may be found in iodized salt. While supplements might be beneficial, taking too much iodine can harm your thyroid.

B12: Because vitamin B12 is exclusively found in animal products, a supplement may be required if you keep a strict vegetarian or vegan diet. This nutrient can be found in nutritional yeast and several fortified breakfast cereals.

Zinc: High-protein animal products are the primary source of zinc, and vegetarians may want to consider taking a zinc supplement.

Whole grains, beans, and lentils are examples of vegetarian sources.

Before starting any new supplements, consult with a certified healthcare expert to ensure they are safe for you.

Diabetes Weight Loss Friendly Grocery Shopping

Now is the time to get into the habit of making a grocery list before you go shopping. It will not only help you plan your meals and avoid unhealthy foods, but it will also save you money.

To begin, prepare a menu for the week. If cooking every day doesn't work for you, try doubling recipes so you have leftovers for later in the week. You can also freeze leftovers to have meals ready for later in the month. As you become more comfortable with your go-to recipes, cooking, and grocery shopping will get easier over time. Here's a categorized list to help you make healthy grocery decisions. Let's get started on your shopping:

Category	Items
Non-starchy vegetables	Kale, Mushrooms, Broccoli Cauliflower, Salad greens, Brussel sprouts, Zucchini, Green beans, Artichoke, Asparagus, Cucumber Bell peppers

Starchy vegetables *(keep portion size small)*	Green peas, Corn, Carrots, Potatoes (white and sweet), Beets, Parsnips, Pumpkin, Winter squash, Yams
Fruits	Berries, Apples, Oranges, Bananas, Watermelon, Pears, Avocado, Tomatoes, Kiwi, Dragon Fruit
Oils, dressings, and spreads	Canola oil, Peanut butter Almond butter, Olive-oil-based unsweetened dressing, Low-sodium barbeque sauce, Low-sodium soy sauce, Local honey Olive oil, Olive oil spray
Beans and legumes	Kidney beans, Pinto beans, Lentils, Black beans, Garbanzo beans
Meats and Eggs	Lean meat: Poultry, including chicken, turkey, and Cornish hen (without skin), Some beef cuts, such as sirloin, flank steak, tenderloin, and chipped beef, Lean pork, Veal, except for veal cutlets

	Wild game, such as venison and rabbit, including pheasant, duck, and goose without skin, Egg or Egg whites, Medium-fat meat (consumption in moderation), Ground beef, chuck steak, and T-bone steak
	Pork chops, loin roast, and cutlets, Lamb, Veal cutlets
	Poultry with skin, Liver, heart, kidney, and sweetbreads
Seafood	Salmon, Tilapia, Cod, Shrimp, Tuna, Sardines
Whole grains	Bulgar wheat, Barley, Farro, Quinoa, Whole grain bread
	Whole wheat pasta, Whole grain cereal (check the added sugar), Oatmeal (consider swapping brown sugar and raisins for cinnamon and berries)
Dairy	Greek yogurt, Low-fat milk
	Low-fat cottage cheese, Low-sodium cheese, like mozzarella

Snack foods	Nuts, such as almonds or almond butter, Vegetable sticks, like celery or baby carrots, Cheese and whole-grain crackers, Popcorn, Chia seed pudding, No-bake energy bites Trail mix, Edamame
Desserts	100-percent fruit popsicles Ice cream sweetened with Stevia (or other low-calorie sweeteners), Low sugar cookies, Dark chocolate, Granola, Frozen and canned foods, Olives, tomatoes, mushrooms, lentils, canned chickpeas, pumpkin, and coconut milk, etc., Frozen vegetables, fruits, meats, etc. Pro tip: You can practically cut the salt level of canned foods in half by rinsing and draining them.

How to Control Your Portion Size

It is essential for everyone to keep track of how much they eat. Paying attention to portion sizes is crucial for everyone, but it's especially important for the 37 million Americans who have diabetes. Portion sizes have gotten warped from actual portions, and we now perceive portions and believe them to be a true serving size. Overeating and weight gain can result from portion distortion, which is especially dangerous for diabetics because more pounds raise their risk of heart disease, stroke, high blood pressure, unhealthy cholesterol, and high blood glucose (sugar). Weight loss and maintenance can also enhance insulin sensitivity. Overeating is bad for all, diabetic or not. You can control your blood sugar and understand portion sizes with the help of these tips.

1. Measure and weigh your food to determine how much you're eating

Many people, diabetic or not, have difficulty estimating portion sizes. We can't be healthy if we consume everything that comes our way; weighing and measuring educate us about portion control. For women and men with diabetes, the recommended daily allowance of total carbohydrates is 45 to 60 g and 30 to 45 g, respectively. So how can you determine whether you're consuming the appropriate amount of food? The following portions, for example, all have 15 g of carbs: 1/3 cup cooked rice, 1 1/2 cup cooked legumes (such lentils, black beans, or garbanzo beans), 1 tennis-ball-sized apple, and 1 (average) slice of bread.

You may measure all of this at home (with measuring cups and spoons) to see what these common portion sizes look like on your plates. However, if you have type 1 or type 2 diabetes and are on insulin, you should use a scale. You can find out how many carbohydrates a food product has by using some scales.

2. Using visual aids, you can estimate portion size when dining out

For instance, 1 cup is around the size of a baseball, and 1 serving of meat, which is approximately 3 ounces (oz), should be equivalent to a deck of playing cards. A 1/2 cup is around the size of a tennis ball and equates to 1-oz equivalents, such as 1 serving of grains like cooked pasta, cooked rice, or cooked oatmeal.

3. Check food labels for calories, serving sizes, carbohydrates, and sodium

As previously stated, it is critical to carefully read food labels while controlling portion sizes. The serving size is the first thing to take note of when reading a food label. Food labels are not always written to be one serving. As a result, if the serving size is higher than one, you'll need to determine how much you're consuming. For example, if the serving size is 5 crackers but you consume 10 crackers, you have to double all of the information: 100 calories turn into 200 calories, 250 mg of sodium turns into 500 mg, and so on. You should also consider how much-saturated fat you consume, as those with type 2 diabetes are at a higher risk of developing heart disease. It's also crucial to keep an eye on your sodium consumption.

For most adults, the American Heart Association recommends eating no more than 2,300 mg per day, with a recommended limit of no more than 1,500 mg per day, and this can be even more significant for people with diabetes. Many people can benefit from reducing their salt intake. Lowering blood pressure also reduces the risk of a heart attack or stroke, both of which are serious complications for diabetics.

4. Request for a doggie bag before you start eating

When dining out, asking for a doggie bag or to-go container is a proven method of practicing portion control. According to one study, women who were given the option to take leftovers ate much less in response to being offered more food. But don't wait until the end of your meal to request a doggie bag. To avoid temptation, request that your server package half of your entrée before it arrives at the table, or cut it in two yourself before you commence to eat. You're more likely to get a proper portion if you're already minimizing what's in front of you. This also prevents you from cleaning your plate, which is detrimental to portion control. When there is food in front of us, we tend to keep munching even when we aren't hungry or because we don't want to waste food. Ordering one entrée to share with a friend or ordering an appetizer instead of an entrée are some strategies to avoid overeating when dining out.

5. Keep a food journal to monitor portions and blood glucose

Keeping a food journal has an additional benefit for someone with diabetes: by recording your intake and blood glucose, you will discover how foods affect your blood glucose. This will only work if you measure your blood glucose in pairs. Take measurements right before and two hours after eating. If you practice this frequently enough, you will learn the optimum foods and quantity sizes for you. Food journaling may also help you lose weight if you're attempting to lose weight. According to one study, the frequency of dietary self-monitoring is highly associated with weight loss.

6. Avoid supersized portions

What exactly is a portion, anyway? In this day and age of oversized meals, it's difficult to tell. In general, restaurant portions are rather large - portion sizes have increased significantly over the last several decades. For example, today's bagels or muffins are frequently at least two portions, yet we tend to eat the entire thing, thinking we've only eaten one serving. Additionally, even if supersized portions are sometimes provided at comparatively modest costs, resist the urge to take a bite just because it seems like a good 1 deal. Supersized meals are high in calories for everyone, not just diabetics. Excessive calorie consumption leads to weight increase, which is a risk factor for both heart disease and diabetes. Furthermore, if you already have diabetes, you are at risk of having your blood sugar levels rise.

7. Be wary of blood sugar boosting drinks

People with diabetes (and even those who do not have diabetes) are far better off avoiding sugary drinks such as soda, juice, sports drinks, sugar-added coffee, alcoholic beverages (such as sugary frozen drinks), sweet tea, lemonade, energy drinks, flavored waters, and sweetened nondairy kinds of milk. You're asking your pancreas to secrete enough insulin to cover the circulating glucose that was just ingested. Since these drinks often lack extra nutrients and fiber, they might create a sharp increase in blood sugar that can be difficult to control if you have diabetes, even if this isn't usually a problem with a typically functioning pancreas. Even worse, when you combine sugary drinks with food, you're taking too many carbs all at once.

Water, flavored water (cucumber melon, mint with lime), unsweetened tea, and sparkling water (sweetened sparkling waters are available, so choose wisely). According to one study, in addition to weight gain, higher consumption of sugar-sweetened beverages is linked to the development of metabolic syndrome and type 2 diabetes. Another study discovered that drinking sugar-sweetened beverages regularly is linked to an increase in insulin resistance and an increased chance of getting prediabetes.

8. Don't be afraid to snack between meals

Think you have to give up snacks because you have diabetes? Quite the reverse. Snacks are crucial during the day to help with overall blood sugar regulation. However, when you eat, is just as essential as what you eat since you want to give your blood sugar ample time to return to normal before eating. Persistently high blood sugar levels can lead to problems. Snacks high in protein can help you satisfy your hunger without raising your blood sugar. If, for instance, you were feeling hungry at 10 a.m. but your schedule time was breakfast at 7 a.m., lunch at noon, snack at 3:30 p.m., and dinner at 7 p.m., I would suggest you have a protein-only snack, which wouldn't raise your blood sugar [two hours before lunch]. A hard-boiled egg, no starchy vegetables with a dip containing plain Greek yogurt, celery, and peanut butter, a low-fat cheese stick, or avocado and tomato are some examples of protein-only snacks. However, there is enough space between meals for your blood sugar to return to normal levels for your 3:30 p.m. snack, so some carbs are okay and may prevent you from overeating at dinner. A half sandwich (on whole-grain bread), an apple (tennis-ball size) with peanut butter, cottage cheese, and pineapple, cheese and whole-wheat crackers, a plain yogurt with fruit mixed in, or a handful of mixed nuts with fruit are all examples.

21-DAY DIABETES WEIGHT LOSS FRIENDLY MEAL PLAN

Learn how to cook the best diabetic friendly meals for weight loss

Week 1

Breakfast: Banana Walnut Smoothie

Ingredients:

- 2 ripe bananas
- 1/2 cup chopped walnuts
- 1 cup Greek yogurt
- 1 cup almond milk
- 1 tablespoon honey
- Ice cubes (optional)

Preparation:

1. Peel and slice the bananas.
2. Blend the bananas, walnuts, Greek yogurt, almond milk, and honey in a blender.
3. Blend until the mixture is smooth.
4. If desired, add ice cubes and blend once more.
5. Pour into glasses; if desired, top with more walnuts.

Nutritional Information (per serving):

Calories: 320 | Protein: 12g | Fat: 18g | Carbohydrates: 35g | Fiber: 5g | Sugars: 20g

Preparation Time: 10 minutes
Number of Servings: 2

Lunch: Grilled Veggies and Hummus Wrap

Ingredients:

- 1 cup mixed bell peppers, sliced
- 1 zucchini, sliced
- 1 eggplant, sliced
- 1/2 cup cherry tomatoes
- 4 whole-grain wraps
- 1 cup hummus
- Salt and pepper to taste

Preparation:

1. Over a medium heat, preheat a grill pan or outdoor grill.
2. Add pepper and salt to sliced vegetables.
3. Grill the vegetables until soft and slightly charred.
4. Warm up the wraps on low heat.
5. On each wrap, spread the hummus.
6. Spread the grilled vegetables on the wraps.
7. Roll the wraps and, if necessary, fasten them with toothpicks.

Nutritional Information (per serving):

Calories: 380 | Protein: 12g | Fat: 15g | Carbohydrates: 55g | Fiber: 12g | Sugars: 8g

Preparation Time: 15 minutes

Cooking Time: 10 minutes

Number of Servings: 4

Snacks: Sliced Bell Pepper and Guacamole

Ingredients:

- 2 bell peppers, sliced
- 2 ripe avocados
- 1 tomato, diced
- 1/4 cup red onion, finely chopped
- 1 clove garlic, minced
- Juice of 1 lime
- Salt and pepper to taste

Preparation:

1. Slice the bell peppers.
2. Wash and mash the avocados in a bowl.
3. Toss in the diced tomatoes, red onion, garlic, lime juice, salt, and pepper. Stir well.
4. Serve the sliced bell peppers alongside guacamole for dipping.

Nutritional Information (per serving):

Calories: 180 | Protein: 4g | Fat: 14g | Carbohydrates: 15g | Fiber: 9g | Sugars: 3g

Preparation Time: 10 minutes
Number of Servings: 4

Dinner: Chicken and Cauliflower Rice

Ingredients:

- 4 boneless, skinless chicken breasts
- 2 tablespoons olive oil
- 1 teaspoon garlic powder
- 1 teaspoon onion powder
- Salt and pepper to taste
- 4 cups cauliflower rice
- 1 cup broccoli florets
- 1 carrot, julienned
- 2 tablespoons soy sauce

Preparation:

1. Prepare the chicken breasts by seasoning them with salt, pepper, onion powder, and garlic powder.
2. In a skillet, over medium-high heat, heat the olive oil.
3. Cook chicken breasts for about 5mins on each side, or until done.
4. Add cauliflower rice, broccoli, carrot, and soy sauce into the same skillet.
5. Stir-fry until the veggies are soft.
6. Over the cauliflower rice, slice the chicken and serve.

Nutritional Information (per serving):

Calories: 420 | Protein: 40g | Fat: 16g | Carbohydrates: 30g | Fiber: 8g | Sugars: 8g

Preparation Time: 20 minutes
Cooking Time: 20 minutes
Number of Servings: 4

Day 2

Breakfast: Protein Pancakes and Mixed Berries

Ingredients:

- 1 cup oat flour
- 1 scoop vanilla protein powder
- 1 teaspoon baking powder
- 1 cup almond milk
- 1 egg
- 1 cup mixed berries (strawberries, blueberries, raspberries)

Preparation:

1. Whisk together the oat flour, protein powder, and baking powder in a mixing bowl.
2. Mix in the almond milk and egg until smooth.
3. Over medium heat, preheat a nonstick pan.
4. Pour the pancake batter into the pan and heat until bubbles emerge on the surface.

5. Cook the pancake until the other side turns golden brown.

6. Serve with berries of your choice.

Nutritional Information (per serving):

Calories: 350 | Protein: 25g | Fat: 8g | Carbohydrates: 45g | Fiber: 7g | Sugars: 8g

Preparation Time: 15 minutes

Cooking Time: 10 minutes

Number of Servings: 2

Lunch: Tuna Niçoise Salad

Ingredients:

- 2 cans tuna, drained
- 4 cups mixed salad greens
- 1 cup cherry tomatoes, halved
- 4 hard-boiled eggs, sliced
- 1 cup green beans, blanched
- 1/2 cup Kalamata olives
- 4 small red potatoes, boiled and sliced
- 1/4 cup Dijon vinaigrette dressing

Preparation:

1. Arrange salad greens in a big bowl.

2. Add sliced potatoes, tuna, cherry tomatoes, hard-boiled eggs, green beans, and olives on top.

3. Drizzle the salad with Dijon vinaigrette dressing.

Nutritional Information (per serving):

Calories: 450 | Protein: 35g | Fat: 20g | Carbohydrates: 30g | Fiber: 8g | Sugars: 5g

Preparation Time: 25 minutes
Cooking Time: 15 minutes
Number of Servings: 4

Snacks: Celery with Cream Cheese

Ingredients:

- 8 celery stalks, cleaned and cut into sticks
- 1/2 cup cream cheese
- 1 tablespoon chopped chives
- Salt and pepper to taste

Preparation:

1. Use the cream cheese to fill the celery sticks.
2. Garnish with chopped chives.
3. Add pepper and salt for seasoning.

Nutritional Information (per serving):

Calories: 120 | Protein: 3g | Fat: 9g | Carbohydrates: 8g | Fiber: 3g | Sugars: 4g

Preparation Time: 10 minutes
Number of Servings: 4

Dinner: Mushroom Skewers and Beef - Mixed Veggies

Ingredients:

- 1 lb. beef sirloin, cut into cubes
- 1 cup mushrooms, cleaned
- 1 red bell pepper, cut into chunks
- 1 yellow bell pepper, cut into chunks
- 1 zucchini, sliced
- 2 tablespoons olive oil
- 1 teaspoon garlic powder
- 1 teaspoon paprika
- Salt and pepper to taste

Preparation:

1. Over medium heat, preheat the grill or the grill pan.
2. Toss in the beef cubes, mushrooms, bell peppers, and zucchini with the olive oil, garlic powder, paprika, salt, and pepper in a large mixing bowl.
3. Thread the beef and vegetables onto skewers.
4. Grill until vegetables are soft and beef is cooked to your taste.

Nutritional Information (per serving):

Calories: 480 | Protein: 35g | Fat: 28g | Carbohydrates: 20g | Fiber: 6g | Sugars: 8g

Preparation Time: 20 minutes
Cooking Time: 15 minutes
Number of Servings: 4

Breakfast: Whole Grain Toast with Egg and Spinach

Ingredients:

- 4 eggs
- 2 cups fresh spinach
- 4 slices whole-grain bread
- 2 tablespoons olive oil
- Salt and pepper to taste

Preparation:

1. In a skillet, over medium heat, heat the olive oil.
2. Put in the spinach and sauté until it is softened.
3. Fry the eggs to your preference in the same skillet.
4. Toast slices of wholegrain bread.
5. Top each toast with sautéed spinach and a fried egg.
6. Add pepper and salt for taste.

Nutritional Information (per serving):

Calories: 320 | Protein: 16g | Fat: 18g | Carbohydrates: 26g | Fiber: 6g | Sugars: 3g

Preparation Time: 15 minutes

Cooking Time: 10 minutes

Number of Servings: 4

Lunch: Basil Salad with Tomato and Mozzarella

Ingredients:

- 2 cups cherry tomatoes, halved
- 1 cup fresh mozzarella balls
- 1/2 cup fresh basil leaves
- 2 tablespoons balsamic glaze
- Salt and pepper to taste

Preparation:

1. Combine the cherry tomatoes, mozzarella balls, and fresh basil in a bowl.
2. Drizzle the salad with the balsamic glaze.
3. Add pepper and salt for taste.
4. Season with salt and pepper.

Nutritional Information (per serving):

Calories: 280 | Protein: 14g | Fat: 20g | Carbohydrates: 12g | Fiber: 2g | Sugars: 6g

Preparation Time: 10 minutes

Number of Servings: 4

Snacks: Greek Yogurt with a Sprinkle of Chia Seeds

Ingredients:

- 2 cups Greek yogurt
- 4 tablespoons chia seeds
- Honey for drizzling (optional)

Preparation:

1. Scoop Greek yogurt into separate bowls.

2. Garnish over the top with chia seeds.

3. If desired, drizzle with honey.

Nutritional Information (per serving):

Calories: 220 | Protein: 20g | Fat: 10g | Carbohydrates: 15g | Fiber: 8g | Sugars: 5g

Preparation Time: 5 minutes

Number of Servings: 4

Dinner: Lemon Herb Roast Chicken with Green Beans

Ingredients:

- 4 chicken thighs, bone-in, skin-on
- 2 tablespoons olive oil
- 1 lemon, juiced and zested
- 2 cloves garlic, minced
- 1 teaspoon dried thyme
- 1 teaspoon dried rosemary
- Salt and pepper to taste
- 1 lb. green beans, trimmed

Preparation:

1. Set oven temperature to 400°F, or 200°C.

2. Combine the olive oil, lemon juice, lemon zest, minced garlic, thyme, rosemary, salt, and pepper in a mixing bowl.

3. After coating the chicken thighs with the lemon-herb mixture, place them on a baking dish.

4. Roast the chicken in the oven until it's thoroughly done.

5. Sauté or steam green beans until they are tender and crispy.

6. Serve the chicken over green beans.

Nutritional Information (per serving):

Calories: 450 | Protein: 30g | Fat: 28g | Carbohydrates: 20g | Fiber: 7g | Sugars: 6g

Preparation Time: 15 minutes
Cooking Time: 40 minutes
Number of Servings: 4

Day 4

Breakfast: Toasty Banny

Ingredients:

- 2 slices of whole-grain bread
- 2 tablespoons of nut butter (almond, peanut, or any preferred type)
- 1 banana, sliced

Preparation:

1. Toast the slices of wholegrain bread till they get golden brown.

2. On each slice, evenly spread the nut butter.

3. Top with banana slices.

Nutritional Information (per serving):

Calories: 300| Protein: 8g| Carbohydrates: 40g| Fat: 14g| Fiber: 6g

Preparation Time: 5 minutes

Cooking Time: 5 minutes

Number of Servings: 1

Lunch - Ground Turkey Breast and Three-Bean Chili

Ingredients:

- 1 lb. ground turkey breast
- 1 can black beans, drained and rinsed
- 1 can kidney beans, drained and rinsed
- 1 can pinto beans, drained and rinsed
- 1 can diced tomatoes
- 1 onion, diced
- 2 cloves garlic, minced
- 1 tablespoon chili powder
- 1 teaspoon cumin
- Salt and pepper to taste

Preparation:

1. Cook ground turkey till browned in a large pot.
2. Stir in the diced garlic and onions and cook until tender.
3. Add beans, diced tomatoes, chili powder, cumin, salt, and pepper to taste.
4. Leave it for 20 to 30 minutes and allow to simmer.

Nutritional Information (per serving):

Calories: 400| Protein: 30g| Carbohydrates: 45g| Fat: 12g| Fiber: 15g

Preparation Time: 15 minutes
Cooking Time: 30 minutes
Number of Servings: 4

Snack: A Handful of Mixed Nuts

Ingredients:

- Mixed nuts (almonds, walnuts, pistachios, etc.)

Preparation:

- Take a handful of mixed nuts.

Nutritional Information (per serving):

Calories: 200| Protein: 6g| Carbohydrates: 8g| Fat: 18g| Fiber: 4g

Preparation Time: 1 minute
Number of Servings: 1

Dinner: Tofu Curry, Brown Rice and Cauliflower Greeny

Ingredients:

- 1 block of firm tofu, cubed
- 1 cup cashews
- 1 head cauliflower, cut into florets
- 1 cup green beans, trimmed
- 1 can of coconut milk
- 2 tablespoons curry powder

- Salt and pepper to taste
- Cooked brown rice for serving

Preparation:

1. Sauté the tofu in a pan until golden brown.
2. Stir in and cook until the cauliflower and green beans are soft.
3. Add the coconut milk, and stir in the curry powder, salt, and pepper to taste.
4. Simmer until the vegetables are tender.
5. Serve with cashews and brown rice.

Nutritional Information (per serving):

Calories: 500| Protein: 20g| Carbohydrates: 40g| Fat: 30g| Fiber: 8g

Preparation Time: 20 minutes

Cooking Time: 30 minutes

Number of Servings: 4

Day 5

Breakfast: Egg and Vegetable Muffin with Zucchini and Feta

Ingredients:

- 6 eggs
- 1 zucchini, grated
- 1 onion, finely chopped

- 1/2 cup feta cheese, crumbled
- Salt and pepper to taste

Preparation:

1. Set the oven to 175°C/350°F.
2. Beat the eggs in a bowl with the feta, onions, zucchini, salt, and pepper.
3. Fill muffin cups with the mixture.
4. Bake until done for 20 to 25 minutes.

Nutritional Information (per serving):

Calories: 250| Protein: 15g| Carbohydrates: 8g| Fat: 18g| Fiber: 2g

Preparation Time: 15 minutes
Cooking Time: 20 minutes
Number of Servings: 3

Lunch: Chicken Caesar Salad and Spinach Wrap

Ingredients:

- 1 grilled chicken breast, sliced
- 2 cups spinach leaves
- 1/4 cup Caesar dressing
- 1 whole-grain wrap

Preparation:

1. Arrange the spinach leaves on the wrap.
2. Next, put the sliced grilled chicken.
3. Pour Caesar dressing on top.

4. Roll the chicken salad wrap and serve it.

Nutritional Information (per serving):

Calories: 400| Protein: 30g| Carbohydrates: 20g| Fat: 20g| Fiber: 5g

Preparation Time: 10 minutes

Number of Servings: 1

Snacks: Sliced Melon:

Ingredients:

- Assorted melon slices (watermelon, cantaloupe, honeydew)

Preparation:

- Cut melons into small, bite-sized chunks and serve

Nutritional Information (per serving):

Calories: 60

Protein: 1g| Carbohydrates: 15g| Fat: 0g| Fiber: 1g

Preparation Time: 5 minutes

Number of Servings: 1

Dinner: Grilled Fish Tacos Topped with Cabbage-Cilantro Slaw

Ingredients:

- 1 lb. white fish fillets
- 8 small corn tortillas
- 2 cups cabbage, shredded
- 1/2 cup fresh cilantro, chopped
- 1 lime, juiced

- 1 tablespoon olive oil
- Salt and pepper to taste

Preparation:

1. Grill fish fillets on the grill until done.
2. Combine the cabbage, cilantro, olive oil, lime juice, salt, and pepper in a bowl.
3. Gently warm the tortillas, assemble the grilled fish, slaw, and tacos.

Nutritional Information (per serving):

Calories: 350| Protein: 25g| Carbohydrates: 40g| Fat: 12g

Fiber: 6g

Preparation Time: 20 minutes

Cooking Time: 10 minutes

Number of Servings: 4

Day 6

Breakfast - Avocado and Berry Smoothie

Ingredients:

- 1 ripe avocado
- 1 cup mixed berries (strawberries, blueberries, raspberries)
- 1 banana
- 1 cup Greek yogurt
- 1 cup almond milk
- 1 tablespoon honey

Preparation:

- Blend all of the ingredients until smooth.

Nutritional Information (per serving):

Calories: 300| Protein: 10g Carbohydrates: 40g| Fat: 15g| Fiber: 8g

Preparation Time: 5 minutes

Number of Servings: 2

Lunch: Turkey Breast and Avocado Wrap:

Ingredients:

- 1/2 lb. turkey breast slices
- 1 avocado, sliced
- 1 whole-grain wrap
- 1/4 cup Greek yogurt
- Lettuce leaves

Preparation:

1. Spread Greek yogurt over the wrap after laying it out.
2. Place lettuce, avocado, and slices of turkey on top.
3. Roll the wrap up and serve.

Nutritional Information (per serving):

Calories: 400| Protein: 30gCarbohydrates: 30g| Fat: 18g| Fiber: 8g

Preparation Time: 10 minutes

Number of Servings: 2

Snack: A Handful of Almonds and Cashews

Ingredients:

- Almonds
- Cashews

Preparation:

- Take a handful of almonds and cashews.

Nutritional Information (per serving):

Calories: 200| Protein: 8g| Carbohydrates: 6g| Fat: 15g| Fiber: 3g

Preparation Time: 1 minute

Number of Servings: 1

Dinner: Pork and Veggie Stir-Fry with Brown Rice

Ingredients:

- 1 lb. pork tenderloin, sliced
- 2 cups mixed vegetables (broccoli, bell peppers, snap peas)
- 2 tablespoons soy sauce
- 1 tablespoon hoisin sauce
- 1 tablespoon sesame oil
- 2 cups cooked brown rice

Preparation:

1. Stir-fry the pork in a pan; place aside.
2. Stir-fry the veggies until they are crisp-tender.
3. Return the pork to the pan and mix in the hoisin and soy sauces.

4. Drizzle sesame oil over top.

5. Serve with cooked brown rice.

Nutritional Information (per serving):

Calories: 450| Protein: 30g| Carbohydrates: 50g| Fat: 15g| Fiber: 8g

Preparation Time: 20 minutes

Cooking Time: 15 minutes

Number of Servings: 4

Day 7

Breakfast: Whole Grain Porridge with Fresh Fruit

Ingredients:

- 1 cup whole-grain porridge
- Assorted fresh fruits (berries, banana slices, etc.)

Preparation:

1. Prepare whole grain porridge as directed on the package.

2. Garnish with fresh fruit.

Nutritional Information (per serving):

Calories: 300| Protein: 8g| Carbohydrates: 60g| Fat: 4g| Fiber: 10g

Preparation Time: 15 minutes

Number of Servings: 2

Lunch: Lentil and Vegetable Soup

Ingredients:

- 1 cup lentils
- 1 onion, diced

- 2 carrots, sliced
- 2 celery stalks, chopped
- 4 cups vegetable broth
- 1 can diced tomatoes
- 1 teaspoon cumin
- Salt and pepper to taste

Preparation:

1. Sauté onions till translucent in a pot.
2. Stir in the diced tomatoes, cumin, salt, pepper, carrots, and celery along with the lentils and vegetable broth.
3. Let the veggies and lentils simmer for some time until they are softened.

Nutritional Information (per serving):

Calories: 350| Protein: 18g| Carbohydrates: 60g| Fat: 2g| Fiber: 15g

Preparation Time: 20 minutes

Cooking Time: 30 minutes

Number of Servings: 4

Snack: Honey Yogurt

Ingredients:

- Greek yogurt
- Honey

Preparation:

1. Spoon the Greek yogurt into a bowl.
2. Drizzle with honey to taste.

Nutritional Information (per serving):

Calories: 150| Protein: 10g| Carbohydrates: 20g| Fat: 5g| Fiber: 0g

Preparation Time: 2 minutes

Number of Servings: 1

Dinner: Grilled Shrimp with Asparagus and Quinoa:

Ingredients:

- 1 lb. shrimp, peeled and deveined
- 1 bunch asparagus, trimmed
- 1 cup quinoa, cooked
- 2 tablespoons olive oil
- Lemon juice, salt, and pepper to taste

Preparation:

1. Cook the shrimp and asparagus on a grill.
2. Mix with the cooked quinoa.
3. Drizzle with olive oil, lemon juice, salt, and pepper to taste.

Nutritional Information (per serving):

Calories: 400| Protein: 25g| Carbohydrates: 40g| Fat: 18g| Fiber: 6g

Preparation Time: 20 minutes

Cooking Time: 15 minutes

Number of Servings: 4

Week 2

Breakfast: Oaty Walnuts and Mixed Berries

Ingredients:

- 1 cup steel-cut oats
- 2 cups water
- 1/4 cup chopped walnuts
- 1/2 cup fresh berries (blueberries, strawberries, raspberries)
- Honey or maple syrup for drizzling (optional)

Preparation:

1. Heat the water in a pot until it boils.
2. Reduce the heat to a simmer and stir in the steel-cut oats.
3. Cook the oats for 20-25 minutes, stirring occasionally, until they reach the desired consistency.
4. Serve with chopped walnuts and fresh berries on top.
5. If desired, drizzle with honey or maple syrup.

Nutritional Information (per serving):

Calories: 300| Protein: 10g| Carbohydrates: 45g| Fat: 10g| Fiber: 8g

Preparation Time: 5 minutes

Cooking Time: 25 minutes

Number of Servings: 2

Lunch: Salmon Salad with Cannellini Beans

Ingredients:

- 2 salmon fillets, grilled or baked
- 1 can (15 oz) of drained and rinsed cannellini beans
- Mixed salad greens
- Cherry tomatoes, halved
- Cucumber, sliced
- Red onion, thinly sliced
- Olive oil and balsamic vinegar for dressing
- Salt and pepper to taste

Preparation:

1. Make tiny flake shapes out of baked or grilled salmon.
2. Combine the cannellini beans, salad greens, cherry tomatoes, cucumber, and red onion in a large mixing basin.
3. Drizzle olive oil and balsamic vinegar over the salad.
4. Serve with flaked salmon on top.
5. For taste, add salt and pepper, mix well, and serve.

Nutritional Information (per serving):

Calories: 400| Protein: 30g| Carbohydrates: 30g| Fat: 20g| Fiber: 10g

Preparation Time: 15 minutes
Number of Servings: 2

Snacks: Sliced Cucumber and Salsa

Ingredients:

- 1 cucumber, sliced
- 1/2 cup salsa

Preparation:

1. Arrange the cucumber slices on a plate.
2. Serve alongside salsa for dipping.

Nutritional Information (per serving):

Calories: 50| Protein: 2g| Carbohydrates: 12g| Fat: 0g| Fiber: 3g

Preparation Time: 5 minutes

Number of Servings: 1

Dinner: Roasted Chicken -Potato- Herbs Vinaigrette Greeny

Ingredients:

- 2 boneless, skinless chicken breasts
- 4 potatoes, quartered
- 1 bunch scallions, trimmed
- Mixed salad greens
- Olive oil, balsamic vinegar, Dijon mustard, fresh herbs (rosemary, thyme), salt, and pepper for vinaigrette

Preparation:

1. Set oven temperature to 200°C, or 400°F.

2. On a baking sheet, arrange the chicken breasts, quartered potatoes, and scallions.

3. Season with salt, pepper, and fresh herbs and drizzle with olive oil.

4. Roast for 25-30 minutes, or until the chicken is done and the potatoes are golden.

5. For the vinaigrette, whisk together olive oil, balsamic vinegar, Dijon mustard, and extra herbs in a small bowl.

6. On a bed of mixed salad greens, place the roasted chicken, potatoes, and scallions. Drizzle the vinaigrette over the salad.

Nutritional Information (per serving):

Calories: 450| Protein: 35g| Carbohydrates: 40g| Fat: 15g| Fiber: 8g

Preparation Time: 15 minutes
Cooking Time: 30 minutes
Number of Servings: 2

Day 2

Breakfast: Strawberry, Peach, and Almond Milk Smoothie

Ingredients:

- 1 cup strawberries, hulled
- 1 peach, pitted and sliced
- 1 cup almond milk

- 1/4 cup almonds, sliced
- Ice cubes (optional)

Preparation:

1. Mix strawberries, peach slices, and almond milk in a blender, add ice cubes if preferred.
2. Blend until completely smooth.
3. Served in a glass cup garnished with sliced almonds.

Nutritional Information (per serving):

Calories: 250| Protein: 8g| Carbohydrates: 30g| Fat: 12g| Fiber: 6g

Preparation Time: 5 minutes

Number of Servings: 1

Lunch: Fresh Herbs and Lentils Stew

Ingredients:

- 1 cup dry lentils, rinsed
- 1 onion, diced
- 2 cloves garlic, minced
- 1 carrot, diced
- 1 celery stalk, diced
- 4 cups vegetable broth
- 2 cups fresh spinach, chopped
- Fresh herbs (parsley, thyme)
- Salt and pepper to taste

Preparation:

1. In a large pot, sauté the onions, garlic, carrot, and celery until tender.

2. Pour in the lentils and vegetable broth. Bring the water to a boil.

3. Reduce the heat to low, cover, and cook for 25-30 minutes, or until the lentils are cooked.

4. Add the chopped spinach and fresh herbs and mix well.

5. Season with salt and pepper to taste. Serve immediately.

Nutritional Information (per serving):

Calories: 350| Protein: 20g| Carbohydrates: 60g| Fat: 2g| Fiber: 18g

Preparation Time: 15 minutes

Cooking Time: 30 minutes

Number of Servings: 4

Snacks: A Bowl of Mixed Berries with Greek Yogurt

Ingredients:

- 1 cup mixed berries (blueberries, raspberries, strawberries)
- 1/2 cup Greek yogurt

Preparation:

1. Combine mixed berries in a bowl.

2. Next, as a dipping for the side, serve with Greek yogurt

Nutritional Information (per serving):

Calories: 150| Protein: 8g| Carbohydrates: 25g| Fat: 3g| Fiber: 5g

Preparation Time: 5 minutes

Number of Servings: 1

Dinner: Herb Garlic Turkey Meatloaf with Mashed Cauliflower

Ingredients:

- 1 pound ground turkey
- 1/2 cup breadcrumbs
- 1 onion, finely chopped
- 2 cloves garlic, minced
- 1/4 cup fresh herbs (parsley, thyme), chopped
- 1 egg
- Salt and pepper to taste
- Cauliflower, boiled and mashed
- Olive oil for drizzling

Preparation:

1. Set oven temperature to 375°F, or 190°C.
2. Combine the ground turkey, breadcrumbs, onion, garlic, fresh herbs, egg, salt, and pepper in a mixing bowl.
3. On a baking sheet, shape the mixture into a loaf.
4. Bake until the internal temperature reaches 165°F (74°C)/ for 45–50 minutes.
5. Serve the turkey meatloaf slices with mashed cauliflower. Drizzle with olive oil to finish.

Nutritional Information (per serving):

Calories: 400| Protein: 30g| Carbohydrates: 30g| Fat: 18g| Fiber: 8g

Preparation Time: 20 minutes

Cooking Time: 50 minutes

Number of Servings: 4

Day 3

Breakfast: Overnight Berry Oats

Ingredients:

- 1/2 cup rolled oats
- 1/2 cup Greek yogurt
- 1/2 cup milk (dairy or plant-based)
- 1/2 cup mixed berries (blueberries, raspberries, strawberries)
- 1 tablespoon honey or maple syrup (optional)

Preparation:

1. Layer rolled oats, Greek yogurt, milk, and mixed berries in a jar or container.
2. Mix thoroughly and refrigerate overnight.
3. Give it a good stir in the morning and if desired, drizzle with honey or maple syrup.

Nutritional Information (per serving):

Calories: 300| Protein: 15g| Carbohydrates: 45g| Fat: 8g| Fiber: 8g

Preparation Time: 5 minutes (plus overnight refrigeration)

Number of Servings: 1

Lunch: Veggie Pita Sandwich

Ingredients:

- Whole wheat pita bread
- Hummus
- Sliced cucumber
- Sliced tomato
- Red onion, thinly sliced
- Feta cheese, crumbled
- Fresh herbs (parsley, mint)

Preparation:

1. Cut the pita bread in half and spread each pocket with hummus.
2. Pack with slices of cucumber, tomato, red onion, crumbled feta, and fresh herb.
3. Serve right away.

Nutritional Information (per serving):

Calories: 350| Protein: 10g| Carbohydrates: 50g| Fat: 12g| Fiber: 8g

Preparation Time: 10 minutes

Number of Servings: 2

Snacks: Whole-Grain Crackers with Low-Fat Cheddar Cheese

Ingredients:

- 8 whole-grain crackers (100%)

- 1-ounce low-fat cheddar cheese

Preparation:

1. Arrange crackers on a plate to serve.

2. Serve with low-fat cheddar cheese slices.

Nutritional Information (per serving):

Calories: 200| Protein: 10g| Carbohydrates: 20g| Fat: 8g| Fiber: 4g

Preparation Time: 5 minutes

Number of Servings: 1

Dinner: Roasted Chicken Breast, Roasted Potatoes, and Roasted Brussels Sprouts

Ingredients:

- 2 boneless, skinless chicken breasts
- 4 potatoes, cubed
- 1 pound Brussels sprouts, halved
- Olive oil
- Paprika, onion powder, salt, pepper and garlic powder

Preparation:

1. Set oven temperature to 200°C, or 400°F.

2. On a baking sheet, arrange the chicken breasts, cubed potatoes, and halved Brussels sprouts.

3. Drizzle with olive oil and season with garlic powder, onion powder, paprika, salt, and pepper.

4. Roast until done to your liking and enjoy.

5. Roast for 30-35 minutes, or until the chicken is done and the vegetables are golden.

Nutritional Information (per serving):

Calories: 450| Protein: 35g| Carbohydrates: 40g| Fat: 15g| Fiber: 10g

Preparation Time: 15 minutes

Cooking Time: 35 minutes

Number of Servings: 2

Day 4

Breakfast: Whole-Wheat, Unsweetened Cereal, Nonfat Milk, Peach, Unsalted Roasted Almonds

Ingredients:

- 1 cup 100% whole-wheat, unsweetened cereal
- 1 cup nonfat milk
- 1 medium peach, sliced
- 1/4 cup unsalted roasted almonds

Preparation:

1. Fill a bowl halfway with cereal.
2. Pour in the nonfat milk, then add the roasted almonds and sliced peaches on top.

Nutritional Information (per serving):

Calories: 350| Protein: 15g| Carbohydrates: 50g| Fat: 10g| Fiber: 10g

Lunch: Turkey Sandwich and Berries

Ingredients:

- Whole-grain bread
- Turkey slices
- Lettuce, tomato, mustard
- Mixed berries (blueberries, raspberries, strawberries)

Preparation:

1. Arrange the turkey slices, whole-grain bread, lettuce, tomato, and mustard on a sandwich.
2. Serve with mixed berries on the side.

Nutritional Information (per serving):

Calories: 400| Protein: 20g| Carbohydrates: 50g| Fat: 12g| Fiber: 8g

Snacks: Hard-Boiled Egg and Unsalted Pretzels

Ingredients:

- 1 hard-boiled egg
- Everything bagel seasoning

- Unsalted pretzels

Preparation:

1. Peel the hard-boiled egg and lightly season everything with bagel seasoning.
2. Serve with unsalted pretzels on the side.

Nutritional Information (per serving):

Calories: 200| Protein: 12g| Carbohydrates: 20g| Fat: 10g| Fiber: 2g

Preparation Time: 10 minutes

Number of Servings: 1

Dinner: Broiled Pork Chop, Brown Rice and Raw Spinach

Ingredients:

- 2 bone-in pork chops
- Unsweetened applesauce
- Brown rice, cooked
- Chicken broth, low-sodium
- Fresh spinach leaves

Preparation:

1. Preheat broiler.
2. Broil the pork chops for 15-20 minutes, or until done.
3. Serve with unsweetened applesauce, cooked brown rice, and a bowl of low-sodium chicken broth on the side.
4. Garnish with fresh spinach leaves.

Nutritional Information (per serving):

Calories: 450| Protein: 30g| Carbohydrates: 40g| Fat: 18g| Fiber: 6g

Preparation Time: 20 minutes

Cooking Time: 20 minutes

Number of Servings: 2

Day 5

Breakfast: Whole Grain Buttermilk Pancakes

Ingredients:

- 1 cup whole-grain flour
- 1 tablespoon sugar
- 1 teaspoon baking powder
- 1/2 teaspoon baking soda
- 1/4 teaspoon salt
- 1 cup buttermilk
- 1 large egg
- 2 tablespoons melted butter
- Cooking spray for the pan

Preparation:

1. Whisk together the whole-grain flour, sugar, baking powder, baking soda, and salt in a large mixing bowl.

2. In a separate bowl, whisk together the egg, buttermilk, and melted butter. Combine thoroughly.

3. Mix the wet ingredients with the dry ones and stir well until just combined. Overmixing is not necessary; a few lumps are fine.

4. Heat a griddle or nonstick pan over medium heat and lightly coat with cooking spray.

5. Pour 1/4 cup batter onto the griddle and cook until bubbles form on the surface, then turn and cook until golden brown.

6. Serve with your preferred toppings, such as maple syrup, fresh fruit, or yogurt.

Nutritional Information (per serving):

Calories: 200| Protein: 7g| Carbohydrates: 30g| Fat: 7g| Fiber: 4g

Preparation Time: 15 minutes

Cooking Time: 15 minutes

Number of Servings: 4

Lunch: Navy Bean and Vegetable Soup with Zucchini and Spinach

Ingredients:

- 1 cup navy beans, soaked overnight
- 1 onion, diced
- 2 carrots, diced
- 2 celery stalks, diced
- 1 zucchini, diced
- 1 cup spinach, chopped

- 2 tomatoes, diced
- 4 cups vegetable broth
- 2 cloves garlic, minced
- 1 teaspoon dried thyme
- Salt and pepper to taste
- Fresh herbs (parsley, dill) for garnish

Preparation:

1. Sauté the onions, carrots, and celery in a large pot until softened.

2. Mix in the garlic, thyme, salt, and pepper. Continue to stir for another minute.

3. Pour in the vegetable broth, tomatoes, zucchini, and soaked navy beans. Allow it to boil.

4. Lower the heat, cover, and simmer for 45 minutes, or until the beans are cooked.

5. Add the chopped spinach and stir until it softens.

6. Season to taste and serve hot with fresh herbs.

Nutritional Information (per serving):

Calories: 250| Protein: 12g| Carbohydrates: 45g| Fat: 2g| Fiber: 12g

Preparation Time: 20 minutes

Cooking Time: 1 hour

Number of Servings: 6

Snack: Nonfat Plain Greek Yogurt with Medium Banana and Chopped Walnuts

Ingredients:

- 1 cup nonfat plain Greek yogurt
- 1 medium banana
- 4 chopped walnuts

Preparation:

Scoop the Greek yogurt into a bowl.

Place the banana slices on top of the yogurt.

Top with chopped walnuts.

Nutritional Information (for the entire snack):

Calories: 250| Protein: 18g| Carbohydrates: 35g| Fat: 8g| Fiber: 5g

Preparation Time: 5 minutes

Number of Servings: 1

Dinner: Salmon with Salad of Niçoise Olives and Fresh Cut Green Beans

Ingredients:

- 4 salmon fillets
- 1 cup Niçoise olives, pitted
- 1-pound fresh green beans, trimmed
- 2 tablespoons olive oil
- Salt and pepper to taste
- Lemon wedges for serving

Preparation:

1. Set oven temperature to 200°C, or 400°F.

2. Add salt and pepper to taste and bake the salmon fillets for 15 to 20 minutes, or until they are cooked through.

3. For 3–4 minutes, blanch the green beans in boiling water until they are crisp-tender. Drain and set aside.

4. Toss the green beans with the Niçoise olives and olive oil in a bowl.

5. Serve the baked salmon on a bed of green beans and olive salad.

6. Before serving, carefully squeeze lemon wedges over the top of the salad.

Nutritional Information (per serving):

Calories: 400| Protein: 30g| Carbohydrates: 10g| Fat: 25g| Fiber: 4g

Preparation Time: 15 minutes

Cooking Time: 20 minutes

Number of Servings: 4

Day 6

Breakfast: Veggie-Loaded Omelet with Summer Squash and Avocado

Ingredients:

- 4 large eggs
- 1/2 cup diced summer squash

- 1/4 cup diced avocado
- Salt and pepper to taste
- 1 tablespoon olive oil
- Fresh herbs for garnish (optional)

Preparation:

1. In a bowl, whisk together the eggs and season with salt and pepper.
2. Over medium heat, heat the olive oil in a nonstick skillet.
3. Add the diced summer squash and sauté until it becomes tender.
4. Cover the squash with the beaten eggs and cook until the edges begin to set.
5. Add diced avocado to one half of the omelet and fold the other half over the top.
6. Cook until eggs are entirely cooked through. If desired, garnish with fresh herbs.

Nutritional Information (per serving):

Calories: 300| Protein: 15g| Carbohydrates: 5g| Fat: 25g| Fiber: 3g

Preparation Time: 10 minutes

Cooking Time: 10 minutes

Number of Servings: 2

Lunch: Fal-Tabbo Whole Grain Pita

Ingredients:

- 1 can (15 oz) chickpeas, drained
- 1/2 onion, roughly chopped
- 2 cloves garlic
- 1 teaspoon ground cumin
- 1 teaspoon ground coriander
- 1/4 cup fresh parsley, chopped
- Salt and pepper to taste
- 4 whole grain pitas
- Hummus and tabbouleh for serving

Preparation:

1. Set oven temperature to 375°F, or 190°C.
2. Combine chickpeas, onion, garlic, cumin, coriander, parsley, salt, and pepper in a food processor. Blend until well combined.
3. Form the mixture into small patties and arrange them on a baking sheet.
4. Bake for 20-25 minutes, or until the falafel is golden brown.
5. Serve in whole-grain pitas with hummus and tabbouleh.

Nutritional Information (per serving):

Calories: 400| Protein: 15g| Carbohydrates: 65g| Fat: 10g| Fiber: 12g

Preparation Time: 15 minutes

Cooking Time: 25 minutes

Number of Servings: 4

Snack: Whole-Wheat Toast and Almond Butter

Ingredients:

- 2 slices of 100% whole-wheat bread
- 1 tablespoon almond butter

Preparation:

1. Toast the whole wheat bread slices.
2. Spread almond butter on each slice evenly.

Nutritional Information (for the entire snack):

Calories: 250| Protein: 9g| Carbohydrates: 30g| Fat: 12g| Fiber: 6g

Preparation Time: 5 minutes

Number of Servings: 1

Dinner: Baked Chicken Parmesan with Parsley

Ingredients:

- 4 boneless, skinless chicken breasts
- 1 cup whole wheat breadcrumbs
- 1/2 cup grated Parmesan cheese
- 1 teaspoon dried oregano
- 1 teaspoon dried basil
- Salt and pepper to taste
- 2 eggs, beaten

- 1 cup marinara sauce
- 1 cup shredded mozzarella cheese
- Fresh parsley for garnish

Preparation:

1. Set oven temperature to 375°F, or 190°C.
2. Combine the breadcrumbs, Parmesan, basil, oregano, salt, and pepper in a bowl.
3. Take the chicken breasts and dip each into the already beaten eggs, then use the breadcrumb mixture to coat them.
4. Bake the coated chicken breasts for 25-30 minutes in a baking dish, or until the chicken is cooked through.
5. Cover each chicken breast with a spoonful of marinara sauce and sprinkle with mozzarella.
6. Bake the chicken for an extra 10 minutes, or until the cheese is melted and frothy.
7. Before serving, garnish with fresh parsley.

Nutritional Information (per serving):

Calories: 450| Protein: 40g| Carbohydrates: 20g| Fat: 20g| Fiber: 4g

Preparation Time: 20 minutes

Cooking Time: 40 minutes

Number of Servings: 4

Breakfast: Mixed Berry Parfait with Nuts and Seeds

Ingredients:

- 1 cup mixed berries (strawberries, blueberries, raspberries)
- 1 cup Greek yogurt
- 1/4 cup granola
- 1 tablespoon mixed nuts and seeds (almonds, chia seeds, flaxseeds)

Preparation:

1. Layer mixed berries in a bowl or glass.
2. Top with a Greek yogurt layer.
3. Over the yogurt, sprinkle the granola.
4. Garnish with a mixture of nuts and seeds.

Nutritional Information (per serving):

Calories: 300| Protein: 15g| Carbohydrates: 40g| Fat: 10g| Fiber: 8g

Preparation Time: 10 minutes

Number of Servings: 1

Lunch: Turkey and Swiss Sandwich on Whole Grain

Ingredients:

- 8 slices whole grain bread
- ½ pound turkey breast slices
- 4 slices Swiss cheese
- Lettuce, tomato, and mustard for garnish

Preparation:

1. Build sandwiches with turkey, Swiss cheese, lettuce, tomato, and mustard between slices of whole-grain bread.

Nutritional Information (per serving):

Calories: 400| Protein: 25g| Carbohydrates: 40g| Fat: 15g| Fiber: 8g

Preparation Time: 10 minutes

Number of Servings: 4

Snack: Baby Carrot Sticks and Hummus

Ingredients:

- 1 cup baby carrot sticks
- 1/4 cup hummus

Preparation:

2. Place the baby carrot sticks on a plate.
3. Serve along with hummus for dipping.

Nutritional Information (per serving):

Calories: 150| Protein: 5g| Carbohydrates: 20g| Fat: 7g| Fiber: 6g

Preparation Time: 5 minutes

Number of Servings: 1

Dinner: Veggie Pizza with Cauliflower Crust

Ingredients:

1. 1 cauliflower crust (store-bought or homemade)
2. 1 cup pizza sauce
3. 1 cup shredded mozzarella cheese

4. Assorted vegetables (bell peppers, mushrooms, onions, cherry tomatoes)

5. Olive oil, salt, and pepper for drizzling

Preparation:

1. Follow the directions for the cauliflower crust to preheat the oven.

2. Evenly spread pizza sauce over the cauliflower crust.

3. On top, sprinkle with shredded mozzarella cheese and arrange assorted veggies.

4. Before drizzling with the olive oil and use with salt and pepper to season it.

5. Bake according to the crust directions, or until the cheese is melted and bubbly.

Nutritional Information (per serving):

Calories: 350| Protein: 15g| Carbohydrates: 40g| Fat: 15g| Fiber: 10g

Preparation Time: 15 minutes
Cooking Time: 15 minutes
Number of Servings: 2

Week 3

Breakfast: Oatmeal with Apple, Cinnamon, and Nuts

Ingredients:

- 1 cup rolled oats
- 1 apple, diced
- 1/2 teaspoon cinnamon
- A handful of mixed nuts (almonds, walnuts, or your preference)
- 2 cups water or milk

Preparation:

1. Place the rolled oats and water or milk in a saucepan and stir gently until combined. Allow it to boil.
2. Lower the heat to a simmer and stir in the diced apples.
3. Stir in the cinnamon and continue to simmer until the oats are creamy.
4. Serve in a bowl with mixed nuts on top.

Nutritional Information (per serving):

Calories: 350, Protein: 10g, Fat: 12g, Carbohydrates: 55g, Fiber: 8g

Preparation Time: 10 minutes
Cooking Time: 15 minutes
Number of Servings: 2

Lunch: Black Eyed Peas and Vegetable Soup

Ingredients:

- 1 cup black-eyed peas (soaked overnight)
- 1 onion, diced
- 2 carrots, sliced
- 2 celery stalks, chopped
- 1 bell pepper, diced
- 3 cloves garlic, minced
- 1 can diced tomatoes
- 4 cups vegetable broth
- 1 teaspoon cumin
- Salt and pepper to taste

Preparation:

1. Sauté the garlic and onions in a large pot until fragrant.
2. Stir in the bell pepper, celery, and carrots, and cook until the veggies are tender.
3. Add the diced tomatoes, vegetable broth, cumin, salt, and pepper, along with the soaked black-eyed peas.
4. Simmer until the peas are soft.

Nutritional Information (per serving):
Calories: 280, Protein: 12g, Fat: 2g, Carbohydrates: 55g, Fiber: 14g

Preparation Time: 20 minutes
Cooking Time: 45 minutes
Number of Servings: 4

Snack: Sliced Oranges

Ingredients:

- 2 oranges, sliced

Preparation:

1. Peel and slice the oranges.
2. You can juice the orange if you desire.

Nutritional Information (per serving):

Calories: 80, Protein: 2g, Fat: 0g, Carbohydrates: 20g, Fiber: 4g

Preparation Time: 5 minutes

Number of Servings: 2

Dinner: Grilled Sausage with Mustard and Green Beans

Ingredients:

- 4 sausages (your choice)
- 2 tablespoons mustard
- 2 cups green beans, trimmed
- Salt and pepper to taste

Preparation:

1. In a grill, gently arrange the sausages and grill until they are well done.
2. Sauté green beans in a pan with salt and pepper to taste until soft.
3. Serve the sausages with mustard on top alongside the green beans.

Nutritional Information (per serving):

Calories: 450, Protein: 18g, Fat: 30g, Carbohydrates: 20g, Fiber: 8g

Preparation Time: 15 minutes
Cooking Time: 20 minutes
Number of Servings: 4

Day 2

Breakfast: Protein Shake with Berries and Spinach

Ingredients:

- 1 scoop protein powder
- 1 cup mixed berries (strawberries, blueberries, raspberries)
- Handful of fresh spinach
- 1 cup water or milk

Preparation:

1. Mix the spinach, mixed berries, protein powder, and water or milk in a blender.
2. Blend until completely smooth.
3. Pour into a glass and drink up.

Nutritional Information (per serving):

Calories: 250, Protein: 25g, Fat: 3g, Carbohydrates: 30g, Fiber: 8g

Preparation Time: 5 minutes
Number of Servings: 1

Lunch: Chicken and Veggie Bowl

Ingredients:

- 2 grilled and sliced boneless, skinless chicken breasts
- 1 cup quinoa, cooked
- 1 cup broccoli florets, steamed
- 1 bell pepper, sliced
- 1 carrot, julienned
- 2 tablespoons soy sauce
- 1 tablespoon olive oil

Preparation:

1. Grill the chicken breasts until they are cooked through, then slice them.
2. Combine the cooked quinoa, grilled chicken, sliced bell pepper, steamed broccoli, and julienned carrot in a bowl.
3. Add a drizzle of soy sauce and olive oil, then toss to mix.

Nutritional Information (per serving):

Calories: 400, Protein: 35g, Fat: 10g, Carbohydrates: 40g, Fiber: 7g

Preparation Time: 20 minutes
Cooking Time: 15 minutes
Number of Servings: 2

Snack: Greek Yogurt with a Sprinkle of Cacao

Ingredients:

- 1 cup Greek yogurt
- 1 tablespoon cacao powder

Preparation:

1. Scoop Greek yogurt into a bowl.
2. On top, sprinkle with cacao powder.

Nutritional Information (per serving):

Calories: 150, Protein: 15g, Fat: 8g, Carbohydrates: 10g, Fiber: 2g

Preparation Time: 5 minutes

Number of Servings: 1

Dinner: Vegetable and Bean Chili

Ingredients:

- 1 can black beans, drained and rinsed
- 1 can kidney beans, drained and rinsed
- 1 onion, diced
- 2 bell peppers, diced
- 2 carrots, diced
- 3 cloves garlic, minced
- 1 can diced tomatoes
- 2 tablespoons chili powder
- Salt and pepper to taste

Preparation:

1. Sauté onions and garlic in a pot until fragrant.

2. Add carrots, bell peppers, beans, diced tomatoes, chili powder, salt, and pepper to taste.

3. Simmer until the veggies are soft.

Nutritional Information (per serving):

Calories: 300, Protein: 15g, Fat: 1g, Carbohydrates: 60g, Fiber: 15g

Preparation Time: 15 minutes
Cooking Time: 30 minutes
Number of Servings: 4

Day 3

Breakfast: Cottage Cheese with Pineapple and Seeds

Ingredients:

- 1 cup low-fat cottage cheese
- 1 cup fresh pineapple chunks
- 2 tablespoons of chia and sunflower seeds

Preparation:

- Combine low-fat cottage cheese, fresh pineapple chunks, and mixed seeds in a bowl and enjoy.

Nutritional Information (per serving):
Calories: 220, Protein: 25g, Fat: 5g, Carbohydrates: 20g, Fiber: 4g
Preparation Time: 5 minutes
Number of Servings: 1

Lunch: Tomato - Cucumber, and Cheese Salad

Ingredients:

- 2 tomatoes, sliced
- 1 cucumber, sliced
- 1 cup cheese cubes (cheddar or your choice)
- Fresh basil leaves
- Balsamic vinaigrette dressing

Preparation:

1. Place slices of tomato and cucumber on a plate.
2. Add the fresh basil leaves and cheese cubes.
3. Drizzle with the balsamic vinaigrette dressing.

Nutritional Information (per serving):

Calories: 250, Protein: 15g, Fat: 18g, Carbohydrates: 10g, Fiber: 3g

Preparation Time: 10 minutes

Number of Servings: 2

Snack: Low-Fat Cottage Cheese with Cubed Cantaloupe

Ingredients:

- 1 cup low-fat cottage cheese
- 1 cup cubed cantaloupe

Preparation:

- Combine low-fat cottage cheese and cubed cantaloupe in a mixing bowl and enjoy.

Nutritional Information (per serving):

Calories: 150, Protein: 15g, Fat: 3g, Carbohydrates: 20g, Fiber: 2g

Preparation Time: 5 minutes

Number of Servings: 1

Dinner: Tofu-Broccoy-Brown Rice

Ingredients:

- 1 block of firm tofu, cubed
- 2 cups broccoli florets
- 1 cup brown rice, cooked
- 2 tablespoons soy sauce
- 1 tablespoon sesame oil
- 2 cloves garlic, minced
- 1 teaspoon ginger, grated

Preparation:

1. Stir-fry tofu cubes in a wok until golden brown.
2. Stir in the broccoli, garlic, and ginger and continue to stir-fry until the broccoli is soft.
3. Add the sesame oil and soy sauce, then toss to mix.
4. Serve with cooked brown rice.

Nutritional Information (per serving):

Calories: 400, Protein: 20g, Fat: 15g, Carbohydrates: 45g, Fiber: 8g

Preparation Time: 20 minutes

Cooking Time: 15 minutes

Number of Servings: 2

Day 4

Breakfast: Tofu and Berry Smoothie with Hard-Boiled Egg

Ingredients:

- 1/2 cup firm tofu
- 1 small banana
- 1/2 cup blueberries
- 1/2 cup strawberries
- 1 teaspoon peanut butter
- 1 cup ice cubes
- 1 hard-boiled egg

Preparation:

1. Place the tofu, banana, ice cubes, blueberries, strawberries, and peanut butter in a blender. Blend until completely smooth.

2. Serve the smoothie in a glass with a hard-boiled egg on the side.

Nutritional Information (per serving):

Calories: 350, Protein: 20g, Fat: 15g, Carbohydrates: 40g, Fiber: 7g

Preparation Time: 10 minutes
Number of Servings: 1

Lunch: Tuna Wrap and Grapes

Ingredients:

- 1 can tuna, drained
- 2 stalks celery, diced
- 1/2 red onion, finely chopped
- 1/2 cup nonfat plain Greek yogurt
- 1 whole-wheat tortilla
- 1 cup grapes, halved

Preparation:

1. Combine tuna, celery, red onion, and Greek yogurt in a mixing bowl.
2. On a whole-wheat tortilla, spread the mixture.
3. Add the halved grape and roll it into a wrap.

Nutritional Information (per serving):

Calories: 400, Protein: 30g, Fat: 10g, Carbohydrates: 50g, Fiber: 8g

Preparation Time: 15 minutes
Number of Servings: 1

Snack: Apple and Low-Fat Cheddar Cheese

Ingredients:

- 1 medium-sized apple
- 1-ounce low-fat cheddar cheese

Preparation:

- Slice the apple and top with a slice of low-fat cheddar cheese. Enjoy!

Nutritional Information (per serving):

Calories: 150, Protein: 5g, Fat: 7g, Carbohydrates: 20g, Fiber: 4g

Preparation Time: 5 minutes

Number of Servings: 1

Dinner: Honey-Mustard Herbed Salmon with Roasted Sweet Potato, Greek Yogurt, and Black Beans

Ingredients:

- 4 salmon fillets
- 2 tablespoons honey-mustard sauce
- 4 medium-sized sweet potatoes, peeled and diced
- 1 cup nonfat Greek yogurt
- 1 can of drained and rinsed black beans (low-sodium)
- 2 cups broccoli florets, roasted with 1 teaspoon olive oil

Preparation:

1. Preheat the oven.

2. Place salmon fillets on a baking sheet, brush with honey-mustard sauce and bake until done.

3. Toss sweet potatoes with olive oil in a separate baking dish and roast until soft.

4. Serve the salmon with roasted sweet potatoes, Greek yogurt, black beans, and roasted broccoli on the side.

Nutritional Information (per serving):

Calories: 500, Protein: 30g, Fat: 20g, Carbohydrates: 45g, Fiber: 10g

Preparation Time: 30 minutes

Cooking Time: 25 minutes

Number of Servings: 4

Day 5

Breakfast: Spinach Omelet with Whole-Wheat English Muffin and Almond Butter

Ingredients:

- 3 eggs
- 1 cup fresh spinach, chopped

- Salt and pepper to taste
- 1 100% whole-wheat English muffin
- 2 tablespoons almond butter

Preparation:

1. In a mixing bowl, whisk together the eggs and the chopped spinach. Add pepper and salt for taste.
2. Pour the egg mixture into a nonstick skillet that has been heated.
3. Cook until the edges get done, then fold in half.
4. Spread almond butter on both halves of the whole-wheat English muffin after toasting them.
5. Serve the omelet alongside.

Nutritional Information (per serving):

Calories: 400, Protein: 20g, Fat: 25g, Carbohydrates: 30g, Fiber: 8g

Preparation Time: 15 minutes

Cooking Time: 10 minutes

Number of Servings: 1

Lunch: Grilled Chicken Salad with Orange and Whole-Grain Crackers

Ingredients:

- 2 grilled chicken breasts, sliced
- Mixed salad greens
- 1 small-sized orange, peeled and segmented
- 8 100% whole-grain crackers

Preparation:

1. Place slices of grilled chicken over a bed of mixed salad greens.
2. Garnish the salad with orange segments.
3. On the side, serve with whole-grain crackers.

Nutritional Information (per serving):

Calories: 450, Protein: 30g, Fat: 15g, Carbohydrates: 50g, Fiber: 8g

Preparation Time: 20 minutes

Number of Servings: 1

Snack: Turkey Sandwich and Orange

Ingredients:

- 2 slices whole-grain bread
- 4 slices turkey breast
- Lettuce and tomato slices
- Mustard or mayo (optional)
- 1 small-sized orange

Preparation:

1. Build the turkey sandwich with bread, turkey slices, tomato, lettuce, and any desired condiments.
2. Serve alongside a small orange.

Nutritional Information (per serving):

Calories: 300, Protein: 20g, Fat: 8g, Carbohydrates: 40g, Fiber: 6g

Preparation Time: 10 minutes

Number of Servings: 1

Dinner: Grilled Sirloin Steak with Baked Potato, Greek Yogurt, Chives, Mushrooms, and Olive Oil

Ingredients:

- 2 sirloin steaks
- 2 medium-sized baked potatoes

- 1 cup nonfat Greek yogurt
- Chopped chives
- Sliced mushrooms
- Olive oil for grilling

Preparation:

1. Grill sirloin steaks till done to your satisfaction.
2. Bake potatoes until they are soft.
3. Add chopped chives and nonfat Greek yogurt on top of the potatoes.
4. In olive oil, sauté the mushrooms until they become soft.
5. Serve the sirloin steaks alongside baked potatoes and sautéed mushrooms.

Nutritional Information (per serving):

Calories: 600, Protein: 40g, Fat: 15g, Carbohydrates: 65g, Fiber: 8g

Preparation Time: 30 minutes

Cooking Time: 20 minutes

Number of Servings: 2

Breakfast: Banana Walnut Smoothie

Ingredients:

- 1 banana
- 1/4 cup walnuts
- 1 cup low-fat milk or almond milk
- 1 scoop protein powder (optional)
- Ice cubes

Preparation:

1. Blend the banana, walnuts, milk, and protein powder in a blender. Blend until completely smooth.
2. Blend again after adding ice cubes.
3. Pour into a glass and drink up.

Nutritional Information (per serving):

Calories: 350, Protein: 15g, Fat: 20g, Carbohydrates: 30g, Fiber: 5g

Preparation Time: 10 minutes

Number of Servings: 1

Lunch: Grilled Veggie and Hummus Wrap

Ingredients:

- 1 whole-grain wrap
- Grilled vegetables (zucchini, bell peppers, eggplant)
- 2 tablespoons hummus

Preparation:

1. Grill the veggies until they get soft.
2. On the whole-grain wrap, spread hummus.
3. Stuff grilled veggies into the wrap.
4. Tightly roll the wrap.

Nutritional Information (per serving):

Calories: 400, Protein: 12g, Fat: 15g, Carbohydrates: 55g, Fiber: 10g

Preparation Time: 15 minutes

Number of Servings: 1

Snack: Dark Chocolate

Ingredients:

- 1-ounce dark chocolate

Preparation:

- Just enjoy a snack of dark chocolate.

Nutritional Information (per serving):

Calories: 150, Protein: 2g, Fat: 10g, Carbohydrates: 15g, Fiber: 3g

Number of Servings: 1

Dinner: Fish Tacos with Grilled Corn

Ingredients:

- Fish fillets (tilapia, cod, or your choice)
- Whole-wheat tortillas
- Cabbage slaw (shredded cabbage, lime juice, cilantro)
- Salsa
- Avocado slices
- Grilled corn on the cob

Preparation:

1. Grill the fish fillets until they are done.
2. Warm the whole-wheat tortillas.
3. Arrange the fish, avocado slices, salsa, and cabbage slaw on the tacos.
4. Serve alongside grilled corn on the cob.

Nutritional Information (per serving):

Calories: 500, Protein: 25g, Fat: 20g, Carbohydrates: 60g, Fiber: 10g

Preparation Time: 25 minutes

Cooking Time: 15 minutes

Number of Servings: 2

Breakfast: Whole Grain Porridge with Tangerines

Ingredients:

- 1 cup whole-grain porridge (oats, quinoa, or a mix)
- 2 tangerines, peeled and segmented

Preparation:

1. Follow the directions on the package to prepare the whole-grain porridge.
2. Top with tangerine segments and serve.

Nutritional Information (per serving):

Calories: 300, Protein: 10g, Fat: 5g, Carbohydrates: 55g, Fiber: 8g

Preparation Time: 15 minutes

Number of Servings: 1

Lunch: Vegetarian Southwest Quinoa Salad with Mixed Greens and Apple Cider Vinaigrette Dressing

Ingredients:

- 1 cup cooked quinoa
- Mixed salad greens
- Sliced cucumbers
- Sliced green and red peppers
- Grated carrots
- 2 tablespoons unsalted sunflower seeds
- Apple cider vinaigrette dressing

Preparation:

1. Mix cooked quinoa, mixed greens, carrots, peppers, cucumbers, and sunflower seeds in a bowl.

2. Add a drizzle of apple cider vinaigrette dressing and mix thoroughly.

Nutritional Information (per serving):

Calories: 450, Protein: 15g, Fat: 15g, Carbohydrates: 60g, Fiber: 12g

Preparation Time: 20 minutes

Number of Servings: 1

Snack: Vanilla Ice Cream with Strawberries and Walnuts

Ingredients:

- 1 cup regular vanilla ice cream
- Sliced strawberries
- 2 walnuts

Preparation:

1. In a bowl, scoop the vanilla ice cream.

2. Serve with sliced strawberries and crushed walnuts on top.

Nutritional Information (per serving):

Calories: 250, Protein: 5g, Fat: 15g, Carbohydrates: 30g, Fiber: 3g

Preparation Time: 5 minutes

Number of Servings: 1

Dinner: Baked Chicken Parmesan with Whole-Wheat Spaghetti and Steamed Broccoli

Ingredients:

- 2 boneless, skinless chicken breasts
- Whole-wheat spaghetti
- Marinara sauce
- Parmesan cheese, grated
- Steamed broccoli

Preparation:

1. Preheat the oven. Brush marinara sauce over chicken breasts and top with grated Parmesan.
2. Bake until the chicken is thoroughly done.
3. To prepare the whole-wheat spaghetti, kindly follow the direction/ preparation method outlined on the package.
4. Serve the chicken over spaghetti with steamed broccoli on the side.

Nutritional Information (per serving):

Calories: 550, Protein: 40g, Fat: 15g, Carbohydrates: 60g, Fiber: 10g

Preparation Time: 30 minutes
Cooking Time: 25 minutes
Number of Servings: 2

Section III

A GUIDE TO HELP YOU START YOUR EXERCISE

Learn simple exercises that are effective and get you going

Create a regular exercise routine to help you control your blood sugar, enhance your heart health, improve your mental health, and achieve and maintain a healthy weight. Even if you understand the need for exercise in diabetes management, getting started might be challenging. Furthermore, once you begin exercising, it might be difficult to stay motivated and continue exercising consistently.

Here's how to get started with a workout routine, overcome typical exercise barriers, and remain active to better manage your diabetes.

1. Consult your doctor: Before starting an exercise plan, get approval from your doctor. If you have joint or muscle issues or are taking medicine for diabetes, high blood pressure, or any other health condition, this is very crucial. In case you have joint or muscle complications, diabetes problems, or both, your doctor will advise you on safe exercise options and how to prevent worsening your particular medical condition. You should also get a dilated eye exam and inform your eye doctor about your physical activity goals. Certain restrictions may apply if you have major alterations in your retina or leakage.

2. Learn how exercising can affect your medication needs: Muscles contract and demand energy when you work out. Glucose provides energy to muscles. The more you work out, the more glucose you burn. At rest, insulin aids in the delivery of glucose to your blood cells; but, during exercise, glucose can reach these cells on its own. The muscles have to restore themselves, and when they are working, they take in more glucose. This process lasts 24 to 48 hours after exercise, making it an excellent method for controlling blood glucose. Furthermore, insulin functions better when you are physically engaged. As a result, your requirement for diabetes medications, as well as other medications, such as high blood pressure treatment, may be reduced. That is why I believe that exercise is the most effective medicine. To prevent low blood glucose (hypoglycemia), you may need to adjust your medication for your workout routine. Also, check with your doctor to see whether your exercise routine will interfere with any other medications you're taking.

3. Evaluate your reasons for not starting a workout routine: Are you worried that once you begin, your blood sugar level will drop too much? Or that you'll be sore afterward because you're out of shape? Everything is superable, even these barriers. Speaking with your doctor beforehand is also important if you're experiencing low blood sugar, since you and your doctor may need to modify the timing or dosage of your medication. Remember that if you begin slowly and progressively increase your workout plan, you will lower the risk of injury and you won't be sore.

4. Understand the many workouts that make up your comprehensive plan: An ideal diabetes exercise plan combines aerobic and strength training. Aerobic workouts include walking, swimming, jogging, hiking, and dancing, as well as the use of cardio machines like an elliptical machine, which can help boost endurance. Strength training (exercises that involve weights, resistance bands, free weights, or suspension ropes) is also important for maintaining or building muscle and increasing metabolism. Stretching exercises and yoga can also help with flexibility.

5. *Choose an achievable goal for yourself:* According to the American Diabetes Association (ADA), people who have type 2 diabetes should develop an exercise plan that includes at least 30 minutes of moderate-intensity exercise five days a week. If you're overweight and need to lose weight, push for 60 minutes of exercise six days a week (split into several bouts per day if necessary). Some people may find these guidelines to be overwhelming: For example, if you've been sedentary, attempting to meet such a goal in the first week is not realistic. Set short-term goals instead; accomplishing each one will give you a sense of success and confidence.

Next, choose an exercise routine that suits your tastes and the time of day that works best for your schedule. A plan that includes a group exercise class at the gym is definitely not the best option for you if you're uncomfortable working out in public. Instead, try doing your workouts at home with fitness apps or by watching online workout videos. A good fitness plan should take into account your strengths, medical conditions, schedule, and likes and dislikes.

6. *Identify what drives you:* Pay attention to the benefits of exercise that are meaningful to you. To be able to change your behavior and continue with your new active lifestyle, you must have positive thoughts about exercise. A workout partner can also encourage, hold you accountable, and make training more enjoyable. Make a plan to meet your relatives or friends at the gym or to go for a walk around your neighborhood after eating.

7. *Pick a pleasant or fascinating activity that you enjoy doing:* To help control your diabetes, you can start with an inexpensive activity and simply move to a different one if you decide to change your mind. That is why brisk walking can often be a good place to start. With a nice pair of sneakers, you can stroll anywhere. Other common activities to explore include dance lessons, yoga, and water workouts.

8. *Schedule exercise:* Just like a doctor's appointment or a lunch date, schedule your workout time in your daily calendar to show that you mean business. If you can't commit to 30 minutes per day, aim for 20. Another way to overcome the time constraint is to divide your activity into 10-minute intervals — research suggests that these breaks may be just as effective as exercising for 30 minutes at a time.

9. Stay hydrated: If you have diabetes and exercise, you must drink plenty of fluids. When you become dehydrated, the concentration of glucose in your blood increases, resulting in high blood glucose, which causes you to urinate more and become dehydrated. Hence, drink before, during, and after workouts. Also, keep a rapid sugar supply on hand - if your blood sugar drops too low (hypoglycemia) while exercising, you'll need an immediate boost.

10. Begin slowly: Once you've devised a workout routine, take it one step at a time. You may feel tired, injured, or discouraged if you overexert yourself. Over time, your endurance will improve. If you've never been active regularly, start with five minutes each day and gradually progress to 10, 15, and so on until you attain your goal. A workout routine may be difficult but not unachievable or overpowering.

11: Listen to your body: If the workout you're doing causes you pain, stop. If the pain or discomfort persists each time you do that exercise, try modifying it or seeking guidance from a physical therapist.

12. Keep track of your progress: Keep track of your physical activities, such as how far you walked, how many miles you covered, and what you did at the gym each time you went. Review the log on a weekly and monthly basis – seeing your progress will encourage and motivate you. Adjust your goals as necessary.

Exercises to Try

Three basic forms of exercise are useful to consider: strength training, cardiovascular exercise, and flexibility training. Remember to consult your healthcare professional before starting or adding on a workout plan.

Beyond just losing weight and getting in shape, exercise is especially important if you have type 2 diabetes. Regular physical activity aids in the management of blood sugar, weight, blood pressure, and cholesterol. This lowers the chance of diabetes-related problems with your heart, eyes, kidneys, and nerves. These are some of the top workouts to attempt.

Workout for Type 1 Diabetes

Running

Running and other aerobic exercises have been shown to be the most beneficial for those with diabetes. It aids in increasing the body's sensitivity to insulin. Running, in a nutshell, serves to reduce the body's requirement for insulin by allowing glucose into cells passively.

This is also one of the reasons it is an excellent exercise for type 2 diabetes. If you are not a runner, start by jogging around the neighborhood and gradually increase the pace and distance.

Swimming

This is another aerobic workout that boosts your heart rate while also being gentle on your joints. Along with Type 1 diabetes, you can attempt this workout on diabetic patients who have diabetic peripheral neuropathy (DPN). Wear an insulin pump before going swimming.

HIIT workout

High-intensity Interval Training (HIIT) is a type of workout that involves short bursts of activity followed by short rest intervals. Jump squats and jumping jacks are the two popular HIIT exercises. This diabetic exercise is beneficial for both Type 1 and Type 2 diabetes patients. Here's an example of a 10-minute workout:

• 10 lunge jumps • 20 pushups • 30 squats • 40 chair dips • 50 mountain climbers

Riding a bike is another beginner-friendly and low-impact activity that improves your heart rate, helps you regulate your blood sugar levels, and has other health benefits. The activity is very enjoyable and allows you to go about town for free. For example, instead of driving everywhere, grab your bike and ride it whenever possible.

Along with getting some vitamin D, you can explore your town and its environs on leisurely bike rides with friends or family.

Workout for Type 2 Diabetes

Walking

Try taking a walk as an alternative to exercising in the neighboring park or gym if you have diabetes. This simple diabetes exercise can be done at home. Five days a week, walk around the block or down the street for at least 30 minutes. Even better if you can switch to brisk walking. Walking is also an effective weight loss activity. You can also try this exercise for type 2 diabetes to reduce stress and enhance your mood.

Pilates

A new study found that Pilates can help with Type 2 diabetes by improving blood sugar levels. Pilates does not require any specific equipment, so you can try it at home. If you are a newbie, sign up at a local Pilates studio or watch online tutorials or books to get the most effective diabetes workout.

Yoga

Yoga is an ancient practice of well-being that provides many health benefits to your body. It can help you lower your blood pressure, blood sugar levels, lose weight, and control your cholesterol levels. In short, it passes as good diabetes exercise.

Furthermore, yoga reduces stress, promotes good rest, and improves body posture to help you live a better life. To begin using yoga as a diabetes exercise, you can learn from yoga-trained professionals or simply register for online yoga courses.

Tai chi

Tai chi also incorporates low-impact moves, meditation, and breathing techniques. This ancient technique improves balance, range of motion, and overall well-being. Incorporating it into a workout plan may also help to reduce your blood sugar.

Others:

Gardening

It is a really good activity that involves lifting, digging, bending, stretching, and using all muscle groups. Having a home garden can also increase your intake of organic fruits and veggies that are grown nearby, which will benefit your health.

Calisthenics workouts

These are strength workouts that involve body weight and are performed at various levels of intensity. Examples include burpees, skipping, jump squats, pull-ups, dips, push-ups, chin-ups, and so on. These exercises target vast muscular groups and are simple to carry out at home.

Dancing

Those who enjoy music can burn fat and calories by dancing. Dancing is a great way to engage in an aerobic workout. There are numerous dance forms to choose from, including Zumba, jazz, belly dancing, and salsa. To make it easier at home, you can also watch YouTube videos.

Strength Training

Resistance training is beneficial for diabetes management because it gives many of the same benefits as aerobics. This form of exercise burns glucose, making it easier to maintain healthy levels. Resistance training additionally builds muscle mass, which improves insulin sensitivity.

Deadlifts

The deadlift is a full-body workout that involves lifting a weight off the floor. By doing this, you train the entire posterior chain, which includes your back, glutes, and hamstrings. Your arms, shoulders, quadriceps, abs, and chest muscle all work hard as well. The deadlift is beneficial since it burns a lot of calories, increases our functional capacity, and can improve insulin sensitivity. Alternatives to regular deadlifts include:

- Sumo deadlifts
- Trap bar deadlifts
- Romanian deadlifts
- Single-leg Romanian deadlifts

Lat Pulldowns

A great exercise for beginners that strengthens your forearms, biceps, and back is the Lat pulldown. The exercise is enjoyable and simple to master. When done correctly, the Lat pulldown strengthens the latissimus dorsi, the largest muscle in the upper body. Your rhomboids, erector spinae, trapezius, infraspinatus, rear deltoids, biceps, and brachialis are also built during Lat pulldowns. Lat pulldowns, like deadlifts, are excellent for burning glucose and enhancing insulin sensitivity.

Bench Press

For good reason, the bench press is one of the most popular resistance workouts. Bench pressing typically builds your chest, shoulders, and triceps. In addition to strengthening us, the exercise enhances your upper body stability. The bench press, like Lat pulldowns and deadlifts, is beneficial because it trains many muscle groups, burns glucose, and leads to optimal insulin sensitivity. If you're new to the gym, you may do variations of the bench press or switch it for easier routines. Examples include:

- Dumbbell bench press
- incline press
- seated machine chest press

Barbell Squats

The barbell squat is commonly referred to as the "King of Exercises." The exercise mainly strengthens our quadriceps, which are the body's second-largest muscle. Squats also build our glutes, train our hamstrings, and engage the upper body, which keeps us stable and upright.

Barbell squats are an excellent whole-body workout that burns a lot of energy and helps keep blood glucose levels within normal ranges. Furthermore, because squats involve so many major muscles in the body, they can help with insulin sensitivity. If barbell squats seem too difficult, you can start with simpler variations, such as:

- Bodyweight squat
- Bodyweight jump squat
- Goblet squat

- Resistance band squat

Other Considerations

If You Have Hypertension

- *You do not have to sit on the sidelines if you have diabetes issues. Your doctor may, however, advise you to avoid certain activities. People with high blood pressure, for example, may be advised to avoid intense activity and excessive weight lifting. Moderate aerobic and strength training, on the other hand, is usually safe.*

If You Have Diabetic Foot Disease

- *Avoid high-impact activities like running or jumping if you have nerve damage in your feet. Moderate, low-impact activities like walking, cycling, and swimming, on the other hand, are normally safe. Chair exercise is one method to stay active if you have a foot disease or injury.*

If You Have Diabetes-Related Eye Disease

- *Avoid strenuous workouts, heavy weight lifting, and high-impact activities if you have diabetic retinopathy, which is damage to the retina of your eye. Also, avoid activities that require you to bend your head down, such as some yoga poses. However, with your doctor's approval, many moderate, low-impact activities are acceptable.*

7-Day Sample Workout Plan for Weight Loss and Diabetes Reversal

Days	Workout I	Workout II
Monday	Barbell squats (10mins)	Treadmill walking/ Pilates (10mins)
Tuesday	Bench pressing (10 mins)	Walking/ Running (10-15mins)
Wednesday	Lat pulldowns (5mins)/ Inverted rows	Bike riding (10mins)/ Swimming
Thursday	Deadlifts (10mins)	Jogging (5mins)
Friday	Lat pulldowns / Bench press (10 mins)	Swimming/ Gardening (10 mins)
Saturday	Barbell squats (10 mins)	Treadmill walking (10 mins)/ Yoga/ Tai Chi
Sunday	Lat pulldowns (15-20 mins), Dance class/ Jogging	Bench press (10mins)

CONCLUSION

This book has taught us several strategies, but overall, you can prevent blood sugar spikes by making modest lifestyle changes like following a low-carb, high-fiber diet as well as avoiding refined grains and added sugars. In addition to helping, you control your blood sugar, regular exercise, maintaining a healthy weight, and drinking plenty of water can all improve your health.

However, if you have any health issues or are taking any medications, consult with your doctor before making any dietary changes.

Making these simple dietary and lifestyle changes is an excellent way to lower the risk of developing insulin resistance or type 2 diabetes for most people. It can be challenging to have to constantly track your diet. Working with a dietitian to create a plan that is personalized to your specific medical condition (including what medications for diabetes you are taking), lifestyle, and personal preferences might be beneficial.

FOOD
AND
WORKOUT
JOURNAL
FOR
YOU

WEEK ONE

		Food	Cal	Pro	Fat	Cbh	Fib
Breakfast	Day 1						
	Day 2						
	Day 3						
	Day 4						
	Day 5						
	Day 6						
	Day 7						
Lunch	Day 1						
	Day 2						
	Day 3						
	Day 4						
	Day 5						
	Day 6						
	Day 7						
Snack	Day 1						
	Day 2						
	Day 3						
	Day 4						
	Day 5						
	Day 6						
	Day 7						
Dinner	Day 1						
	Day 2						
	Day 3						
	Day 4						
	Day 5						
	Day 6						
	Day 7						
	Meal Sub Total						

Week 1 Continued

		Time	Type of Workout
	Day 1		
	Day 2		
	Day 3		
Exercise	Day 4		
	Day 5		
	Day 6		
	Day 7		

Thoughts for the Week

Week 1 Summary	☐ Bad		☐ Good		☐ Excellent
Did I meet my goal this week?		Yes ☐		No ☐	

NB: *You can include the time you take each meal beside the food column. This may help you track and study any pattern of blood sugar spike you experience.*

Cal: Calories| Pro: Protein| Cbh: Carbohydrate| Fib: Fiber

Date:

WEEK TWO

		Food	Cal	Pro	Fat	Cbh	Fib
Breakfast	Day 1						
	Day 2						
	Day 3						
	Day 4						
	Day 5						
	Day 6						
	Day 7						
Lunch	Day 1						
	Day 2						
	Day 3						
	Day 4						
	Day 5						
	Day 6						
	Day 7						
Snack	Day 1						
	Day 2						
	Day 3						
	Day 4						
	Day 5						
	Day 6						
	Day 7						
Dinner	Day 1						
	Day 2						
	Day 3						
	Day 4						
	Day 5						
	Day 6						
	Day 7						
	Meal Sub Total						

Week 2 Continued

		Time	Type of Workout
	Day 1		
	Day 2		
	Day 3		
Exercise	Day 4		
	Day 5		
	Day 6		
	Day 7		

Thoughts for the Week

Week 2 Summary	☐ Bad	☐ Good	☐ Excellent
Did I meet my goal this week?	Yes ☐	No ☐	

Cal: Calories| Pro: Protein| Cbh: Carbohydrate| Fib: Fiber

Date:

WEEK THREE

		Food	Cal	Pro	Fat	Cbh	Fib
Breakfast	Day 1						
	Day 2						
	Day 3						
	Day 4						
	Day 5						
	Day 6						
	Day 7						
Lunch	Day 1						
	Day 2						
	Day 3						
	Day 4						
	Day 5						
	Day 6						
	Day 7						
Snack	Day 1						
	Day 2						
	Day 3						
	Day 4						
	Day 5						
	Day 6						
	Day 7						
Dinner	Day 1						
	Day 2						
	Day 3						
	Day 4						
	Day 5						
	Day 6						
	Day 7						
	Meal Sub Total						

Week 3 Continued

		Time	Type of Workout
Exercise	Day 1		
	Day 2		
	Day 3		
	Day 4		
	Day 5		
	Day 6		
	Day 7		

Thoughts for the Week

Week 3 Summary	☐ Bad	☐ Good	☐ Excellent
Did I meet my goal this week?	Yes ☐	No ☐	

Cal: Calories| Pro: Protein| Cbh: Carbohydrate| Fib: Fiber

Date:

WEEK FOUR

		Food	Cal	Pro	Fat	Cbh	Fib
Breakfast	Day 1						
	Day 2						
	Day 3						
	Day 4						
	Day 5						
	Day 6						
	Day 7						
Lunch	Day 1						
	Day 2						
	Day 3						
	Day 4						
	Day 5						
	Day 6						
	Day 7						
Snack	Day 1						
	Day 2						
	Day 3						
	Day 4						
	Day 5						
	Day 6						
	Day 7						
Dinner	Day 1						
	Day 2						
	Day 3						
	Day 4						
	Day 5						
	Day 6						
	Day 7						
	Meal Sub Total						

Week 4 Continued

		Time	Type of Workout
Exercise	Day 1		
	Day 2		
	Day 3		
	Day 4		
	Day 5		
	Day 6		
	Day 7		

Thoughts for the Week

Week 4 Summary	☐ Bad	☐ Good	☐ Excellent
Did I meet my goal this week?	Yes ☐	No ☐	

Cal: Calories| Pro: Protein| Cbh: Carbohydrate| Fib: Fiber

Date:

Made in the USA
Middletown, DE
14 December 2024

66966977R00106